AS AT THE BEGINNING

By the same author:

POWER FOR THE BODY OF CHRIST

AS AT THE BEGINNING

The Twentieth Century Pentecostal Revival

by

MICHAEL HARPER

LOGOS INTERNATIONAL
Plainfield, N.J.

LOGOS INTERNATIONAL
185 North Ave.
Plainfield, N.J. 07060

AUTHOR'S PREFACE

THIS book is neither a theological nor historical text-book. I have simply taken a few of the more important strands of a much more complicated affair, and tried to weave them into a coherent pattern. I believe there are many who want to know about this pattern of events, incomplete though it is, and to assess its relevance to the healthy life of the Church and its members today.

A wrong impression may be gained by the prominence given to events which have taken place in the United States. This is not an American affair alone—it is affecting churches throughout the world. The need for fresh power from God is common to Christians everywhere, and God's answer is the same—"you shall receive power *when the Holy Spirit is come upon you*".

The main theological issues are touched on, but I have written more fully on these in a booklet entitled *Power for the Body of Christ* (Fountain Trust, 1964).

I should like to thank the Editors of *Trinity* and *Voice* for permission to quote extensively from these magazines; also, Donald Gee for his help in a number of ways and his permission to quote from his book *The Pentecostal Movement,* also George Allen & Unwin and Mr. James Salter for their permission to use material from *The Pentecostal Movement* by Nils Bloch-Hoell and *Smith Wigglesworth, Apostle of Faith* by Stanley Frodsham in Chapters 4 and 5 respectively. All other acknowledgements of sources are made at the end of the book.

MICHAEL HARPER

CHRONOLOGICAL GUIDE

Justin Martyr (*c.* 100–165): early Christian apologist.

Irenaeus (*c.* 130–200): Bishop of Lyons and theologian.

Montanism: an ecstatic movement which began in the Church about A.D. 170.

Tertullian (*c.* 160–220): one of the greatest theologians of the patristic period. He became an ardent Montanist.

Cyril of Jerusalem (*c.* 315–386): Bishop of Jerusalem and a strong opponent of Arianism.

Chrysostom (*c.* 347–407): Bishop of Constantinople. A brilliant preacher and reformer. Deposed by his enemies.

Augustine of Hippo (354–430): Bishop of Hippo and theologian.

Francis Xavier (1506–1552): one of the greatest Christian missionaries of all time. He planted churches in India, Japan and China, where he died.

John Owen (1616–1683): Puritan divine. He was Dean of Christ Church, Oxford, and Vice-Chancellor of the University.

Pascal (1623–1662): French theologian and Jansenist.

Jansenism: a 17th century movement which began in France and spread elsewhere in Europe, and which stressed grace and moral rigorism. Condemned as a heresy by the Papacy.

Jonathan Edwards (1703–1758): an American philosopher and theologian whose church in Northampton, Mass. experienced a revival during his ministry, which he defended from its many critics.

Charles Simeon (1759–1836): a Fellow of King's College, and Vicar of Holy Trinity, Cambridge, for fifty-three years. Leader of the Evangelical Revival.

Curé D'Ars (1786–1859): a simple, illiterate French priest who had a remarkable charismatic ministry.

Edward Irving (1792–1834): a brilliant Scottish preacher, who helped to found the Catholic Apostolic Church.

CONTENTS

11

"As I began to speak, the Holy Spirit fell on them *just as on us at the beginning* . . . if then God gave the same gift to them as He gave to us when we believed in the Lord Jesus Christ, who was I that I could withstand God?" When they heard this they were silenced. And they glorified God. . . .

Acts 11:15, 17–18.

INTRODUCTION

IT is not far from Azusa Street in Los Angeles to the fashionable suburb of Van Nuys. If the highway is not too crowded you can do it in about thirty minutes. There is very little in common between the two, yet there is a fascinating historical connection—and on this hangs a tale.

The beginning of this religious story is difficult to discover. It is rather like a great river, whose source can be traced back to any one of hundreds of tiny streams in the mountains. So it is with Pentecostalism. But it does appear that the movement was born, if anywhere at all, in an old dilapidated building in Azusa Street, Los Angeles. That was in 1906. The building has long since been pulled down.

Almost exactly fifty years later a similar movement emerged in a very different milieu—in the Episcopal Church of America and other big denominations. The genesis of this movement, like the earlier one, is difficult to trace accurately, but it came into the open and received world-wide publicity at St. Mark's Church, Van Nuys, in 1960.

This is the story of an orthodox Christian movement. It began in the churches and was largely ignored or rejected. It became more than another denomination—a third force in Christianity. Now it is reappearing in the churches. It is mushrooming all over the world, sometimes in very unlikely places. It is a talking-point wherever you go in Christian circles.

In this book an attempt is made to trace the intricate story. It has been impossible to give a comprehensive account. However, if only the headlines are read, at least it will give some indication of what the news is all about. In the first part of the book a short account is given of the events in church history leading to the Pentecostal revival at the beginning of this century. Then there is an account

13

of the beginnings in America. After that follows a description of how the movement spread to Europe and later to this country.

In the second part of the book an attempt is made to tell the story of the beginning of the second wave of the movement—inside not outside the historic churches. Here it has been quite impossible to cover the whole ground. We have only been able to give a series of impressions from which certain trends can be evaluated.

In the final section a serious attempt is made to assess all this. It is clear that there are dangers in this subject. It is one thing to talk about electricity or to read books on the subject, but it is another to have to carry out tests with live power. This aspect needs to be remembered. Anyone who rushes into this subject without taking the appropriate precautions is acting irresponsibly.

This section should be read carefully. This is not something to "try out" in one's church, as one might try a stewardship campaign or even an evangelistic mission. The Church desperately needs power today. But power is dangerous; if it gets into the hands of reckless people it can sabotage the Church's life. There is need for clear discernment. Even if you skip the rest of the book, *do not skip lightly through this section*.

Dr. Carl Henry has written: "In twentieth century Christianity the Holy Spirit is still a displaced person.... Whenever the Church makes the Spirit of God a refugee, the Church, not the Spirit, becomes the vagabond."

The Pentecostals, for all their faults, are a body of Christians who have sought to restore the Holy Spirit to His ordained ministry in the Body of Christ. There has been fanaticism and sometimes gross excesses. But their success, particularly in missionary work, can be attributed to this factor more than any other. We, in the churches, who have tended to neglect and quench the Holy Spirit, will be well advised to learn what lessons we can from their example and experience. But better still, discover the secret straight from the New Testament and see it work "as at the beginning".

14

PART ONE

THE WIND BLOWETH

CHAPTER ONE

FROM THE BEGINNING

SHARPEVILLE, Little Rock, Smethwick, Selma are familiar place names. They stand in our day for the race problem—one of the big issues facing mankind. But the world was no different in this respect in Bible days. The Jews, for instance, had no dealings with the Samaritans and there was an even greater race barrier between Jews and Gentiles.

One of the most impressive results of the advent of the Holy Spirit was the breaking of this race barrier. It was the Caesarea incident which did it. All the earliest Christians were Jews by nature. Their prejudice was so deep that they preached only to their own race. Then the Holy Spirit led Peter to a group of Gentiles in a house in Caesarea. In the middle of Peter's talk the Holy Spirit came upon the listeners and they began to speak in other languages under the power of the Spirit. Peter immediately realised that God had given these Gentiles the same gift as He had given them on the Day of Pentecost, so he went ahead and baptised them.

He was hauled over the coals by the church in Jerusalem for doing such a presumptuous thing. These Gentiles had not even become Jews. But Peter "blamed" the Holy Spirit for what had happened.

"As I began to speak," he said, "the Holy Spirit fell on them *just as on us at the beginning....* If then God gave the same gift to them as he gave to us when we believed in the Lord Jesus Christ, who was I that I could withstand God?" (Acts 11: 15, 17).

Peter's critics were silenced. A race barrier had been broken by the Holy Spirit.

We see here the hint of a recurring pattern. There is a further instance of it when Paul arrived in Ephesus and quizzed a small group of disciples. They had been inadequately taught by Apollos, who had told them nothing about the Holy Spirit. Paul gave them proper Christian baptism and immediately laid hands on them. The Holy Spirit came upon them "as at the beginning".

When things are going badly it is only natural to want to start all over again. If the foundations are unsound the whole building will be affected. In the "religionless Christianity" club there is this same urge. In *Soundings*, for example, there is an article by H. E. Root entitled "Beginning all over again". Throughout the history of the Christian Church there has been this instinctive desire to go back to square one and start again. When Billy Graham was once criticised for taking the Church back fifty years, he complained afterwards, "Why, I'm trying to take the Church back 1900 years."

Again and again there has been this desire to return to the shining certainties and primitive simplicity of the age of the apostles. The story of the early Church, as related in the Acts of the Apostles, is a remarkable mixture of human weakness and spiritual power. It all rings true. Here are no supermen defying Church and State with calm logic and intellectual know-how. But there is that element of the supernatural that keeps on cropping up. Here we see a Church of nobodies equipped with gifts of discernment and power of an unusual nature. Peter sees through the deceit of a married couple who have lied to him. Stephen's face shines like an angel as he is dragged into court, later to die by stoning. Paul is supernaturally led and guided. He sees visions and has dreams. Prison doors open, the dead are raised to life, the crippled walk, the blind see. Prophecies warn the Church of impending disaster. This seems to have been normal Christianity. No wonder the Church thrived— and suffered persecution.

Corinth was a pretty seamy city—worse than most. But there was a church there and Paul seems to have corresponded with it a number of times. We still have two of these letters. It does not appear to have been a very healthy church, but in spite of this they were not lacking in spiritual gifts. They seemed to have been rather too keen on one of them, speaking in tongues, and Paul carefully corrects this wrong emphasis; but he urges them to con-

18

tinue to exercise the gifts the Holy Spirit had given them. There is no suggestion that Paul was handling an unusual subject, and there is every indication to suppose that these gifts and manifestations were part and parcel of church and missionary activity in New Testament times.

It is equally clear that this kind of thing continued after the death of the apostles. Irenaeus, writing at the end of the second century, speaks of those who prophesy and have visions. Also he refers to a continuing healing ministry and even the raising of the dead. He tells too of those who "through the Spirit do speak all kinds of languages and bring to light for the general benefit the hidden things of men and declare the mysteries of God".

Even in those early days there were some claiming that these gifts became extinct with the death of the last apostle. Justin Martyr flatly contradicted this assertion. "It is possible now to see among us women and men who possess gifts of the Spirit of God."

But it is possible that at this early stage the rot was already setting in, which led eventually to the temporary cessation of these gifts. The process was accelerated by the over-zealous activities of the Montanists. These were a group which became quite numerous in the Church at that time, claiming to possess the power of the Spirit in an unusual way. They were probably provoked by the increasing formality of the Church—but tended increasingly to fanaticism and frightened the Church into soft-pedalling on the supernatural and asserting its authority. But there was much that was good in this movement, and one of the greatest contemporary church leaders, Tertullian, became a member of it towards the end of his life. He speaks of all the gifts of the Spirit being operative in the Church in his day. One of the most heroic of Christian martyrs—Perpetua—was a Montanist, and many of them proved to be courageous missionary pioneers.

But the gifts did finally disappear from the pages of church history. There have been many explanations for the disappearance. John Wesley was adamant in his opinion of the matter: "The causes of their decline was not as has been vulgarly supposed because there is no more need for them, because all the world were become Christians ... the real cause was: the love of many, almost all Christians so called, was waxed cold ... this was the real cause why the extraordinary gifts of the Holy Spirit were no longer to be found in the Christian Church: because the Christians were turned heathen again and had only a dead form left."

But by the time of Augustine and Chrysostom at the end of the fourth century, the main view of the Church was that the gifts had been given for the founding of the Church and had been withdrawn when they were no longer necessary. It was a convenient alibi to account for their absence in an increasingly institutionalised Church. But they continued without interruption in the Eastern Church.

John Wesley's is one of a number of explanations for this state of affairs. Another would seem to be the increasing emphasis on intellect and reason, which meant that the Church regarded with suspicion anything which could not be rationally explained. "Speaking in tongues", for example, was treated as evidence of demon-possession. For all we know many a true Christian may have perished in the ruthless persecution of witchcraft in the Middle Ages. The healing ministry of the Church virtually disappeared too at this time.

As one might expect, it was at the Reformation that we again see glimpses of light on this subject. Sauer in his *History of the Christian Church* tells that Martin Luther was endowed with all the gifts of the Spirit. Certainly he experienced the supernatural in a remarkable way. We see for instance his faith in divine healing in a letter written in 1545 to a friend asking advice about a sick person: "When you depart lay your hands upon the man again and say, 'These signs shall follow them that believe; they shall lay hands on the sick and they shall recover.'"

There is a record also of St. Francis Zavier speaking languages he had never learnt while on his missionary journeys.

So from time to time, increasing in frequency, the gifts of the Spirit were reappearing throughout the period from the Reformation to the present day. There were widespread and remarkable manifestations in the Cevennes in the eighteenth century among the persecuted Huguenots, which John Wesley seemed to know all about, and also among the Jansenists in France later that century. The brilliant philosopher Pascal was attracted to this group, which all goes to show that, if you add also the names of Paul and Tertullian, these manifestations seem at times to attract intellectual giants, though the view is often taken that these gifts of the Spirit are only meant for the immature.

Some of the early Quakers "spoke in tongues", as did one of Wesley's best-known preachers—Thomas Walsh. He wrote in his diary on March 8th, 1750: "This morning the Lord gave me a language I knew not of, raising my soul to Him in a wondrous manner."

During the nineteenth century there was a quickening of the pace. A great deal of attention has been given to the movement associated with Edward Irving and its unfortunate accompaniments. The wildest fanaticism spoiled what could have been a movement of rich blessing to the churches. But there were many other occurrences devoid of the unfortunate overtones associated with the Irvingites. There was, for instance, a most significant movement in Russia in the middle of the nineteenth century. One fascinating aspect of this is recorded later in this book. In the United States at different times during this century there were scattered instances. There were occasions too during the ministry of D. L. Moody when "speaking in tongues" took place. In the Roman Catholic Church there was a growing interest at the beginning of the century until it was suppressed. This was provoked by the publication in 1812 posthumously of a long rambling book by a South American Jesuit called Lacunza. It was called *The Coming of the Messiah in the Glory and Majesty*. It was later to be translated into English by Edward Irving.

The Cure d'Ars is another prominent person in the nineteenth century who almost certainly spoke in tongues, as this extract from his life story shows: "Soeur Marie Françoise came to his confessional in Holy Week, either 1849 or 1850. When she had finished her confession, she said to him: 'What does God want of me, Father?' 'Ah my child,' said the frail sweet voice behind the grille. And then for the space of five minutes he seemed to be talking to himself, in an unknown tongue. Anyway, she did not understand it. 'Astounded, I looked at his face. He seemed beside himself. I thought he was seeing God. Judging myself unworthy of remaining in the presence of so great a saint, I withdrew very much afraid.'"[1] As the Curé d'Ars was an illiterate man knowing only French and Latin it is quite clear that he must on this occasion have spoken in a language which the Holy Spirit gave him.

Towards the end of the nineteenth century there was a growing sense of expectancy in certain quarters that the world was about to experience another revival. Large numbers of Christians began to pray for this. In the middle of the century a very remarkable revival had broken out in the United States, which had later spread to Ireland and other parts of Britain. The flames were fanned by the efforts of Moody and Sankey and later by Torrey and Alexander. But people were expecting much more to come. It was in this setting that the events we are about to record took place. Those concerned were almost entirely drawn from the ranks of what we might call the "Holiness Movement". This movement was stimulated by the chaotic conditions in the United States following the Civil War. Some of those involved were Methodists, roughly following John Wesley's teaching on holiness. Others were members of the Salvation Army, which had just been founded by William Booth. Others still were associated with the Keswick Convention Movement. Within these groups there were people who began to see that holiness was not enough, that although they needed God's power to be holy, yet in the New Testament God's power was also given to the Church that signs and wonders might be done in the name of Christ. Or in other words there were Christians who wanted to get right back to the early Church's experience of power and live again "as at the beginning". By 1900 the wheels of this revival were beginning to turn.

CHAPTER TWO

BORN IN A STABLE

THE Pentecostal Movement was born in a stable. So was Christianity. Many of the great movements which have shaken a Church which has either grown fat and indolent with prosperity or sterile through formalism have had humble origins. The Reformation was sparked into life in a very unpretentious church in Wittemberg. Here the monk Martin Luther nailed his ninety-five theses to the door of the church on the eve of All Saints' Day—his first act of open defiance against the corruption of the papacy. D'Aubigné has described the church as "an ancient wooden chapel, whose walls, propped up on all sides, were falling into ruin". The pulpit, where Luther thundered his revolutionary sermons, was "made of planks, and three feet high". In England the Reformers were meeting secretly in the White Horse Inn in Cambridge. The Church has seldom reformed itself, but at most times in its history, especially in times of spiritual decline, it has nurtured its revolutionaries who plot its renewal. The Holy Club at Oxford, where the Wesleys and Whitefield met with their discontented friends, was hardly part of the Establishment, and John Wesley, the greatest English revivalist of all times, did not receive his transforming spiritual experience from the hands of a bishop in ordination, but in a dingy room in Aldersgate Street as the Preface to Luther's commentary on the Epistle to the Romans was being read.

The Church tends to honour its revolutionary sons and daughters when they are safely buried. It burns its saints at the stake and then canonises them, as with Joan of Arc. It closes the doors of its churches to its prophets and then builds monuments to them and fills its hymn-books with their compositions, as it did to the Wesleys. It prefers dead saints to living revolutionaries. Human nature has not changed very much since Christ charged the religious leaders of His day with doing this same thing. "You build the tombs of the prophets and adorn the monuments of the righteous, saying, 'If we had lived in the days of our fathers we would not have taken part with them in shedding the blood of the prophets.' Thus you witness against yourselves that you are sons of those who murdered the prophets ... therefore I send you prophets and wise men and scribes, some of whom you will kill and crucify and some you will scourge in your synagogues and persecute from town to town . . ." (Matt. 23: 29–31, 34).

The house in Azusa Street where the Pentecostal Movement was born had been used at one time as a livery stable. Ironically enough, near by was a tombstone factory. The old stable had also served as a Methodist chapel and a lumber yard; it had been damaged by fire and abandoned. Man had no use for it, but God was to choose it as the birthplace of a revolution. Before we follow the strange events which were to take place in the heart of the Negro quarter at 312 Azusa Street in the year 1906, we need to retrace our steps and discover what led up to them.

"There is nothing new under the sun," says the preacher. The doctrines which appear novel and revolutionary in one age may be commonplace in another. The shattering discovery by Luther, for instance, that a man cannot get right with God by his own efforts at good behaviour, but by faith alone, is basic New Testament doctrine. The early Christians would have considered it the height of folly to try to please God in any other way than by appropriating the promise of God by faith. Wesley's appeal to holiness certainly jolted the voluptuousness of Church and State in his day, but it was straight from the text-book, so to speak. The apostles' eyebrows would have been raised in surprise if anyone had dared to suggest otherwise.

So it was at Azusa Street, when men and women came from all over the world to receive what the Bible calls "the Baptism in the Spirit" and "speaking in tongues". We need to remember that the apostle Paul registered surprise when he found some disciples who hadn't even heard of the Holy Spirit. Without delay, after baptising them in water, we find him laying hands on them and they are speaking in tongues as the Holy Spirit comes upon them. St. Paul apparently regarded this as all in the day's work—nothing unusual or revolutionary. But when the same thing happens two thousand years later it causes a theological earthquake and the Church tries to get it out of its system.

But as we have already seen, this was not the first time that speaking in tongues had reappeared in the Christian Church since the days of the apostles. Up to the beginning of the fourth century there are occasional references to this gift, together with the other gifts of the Holy Spirit which were mentioned by St. Paul in 1 Corinthians 12, and which apparently had a vital place in the life of the early Church. But there are then definite signs of its increasing scarceness until in the fourth century it seems to disappear altogether from the records of church history, together with a great deal more of essential Christianity. From the fourth century until our story begins at the turn of this century we seem to be chasing a "will o' the wisp", which reappears at odd times without achieving much prominence.

The Pentecostal child was brought up in the nursery of the Holiness Movement, from which it acquired so much of its teaching—and also, strangely enough, a great deal of its persecution. Methodism, and its various ancestors in the Moravian sects, had always taught both the decisiveness of the conversion experience and also of a further experience, variously called "entire sanctification", "holiness", "perfect love", "the second blessing" and later "the Baptism in the Spirit". It was largely from this rock that the Pentecostal stone was hewn. As we shall see, most of the movement's pioneers were either Methodists, Salvationists or from the other Holiness groups. In the nineteenth century the Holiness Movement thrived both in America and Great Britain. Men such as Charles Finney, D. L. Moody and R. A. Torrey had great influence on both sides of the Atlantic and consistently taught a further experience for Christians which they called "the Baptism in the Spirit". From time to time, too, speaking in tongues took place in the meetings. For instance in 1873 D. L. Moody held a campaign in Sunderland, and Robert Boyd wrote about his visit: "When I got to the rooms of the Y.M.C.A. I found

25

the meeting on fire. The young men were speaking in tongues and prophesying. What on earth did it mean? Only that Moody had been addressing them that afternoon."

So we see that these gifts and experiences were not new to the Church at the dawn of this century. What was new was the linking of speaking in tongues with the experience of the Baptism in the Holy Spirit. It was this which sparked off the Pentecostal revival.

In the autumn of 1900 the Bethel Bible College was opened in Topeka, Kansas. The founder and first principal was a Methodist evangelist called Charles Parham. The students, twelve of whom were ministers, were offered board and instruction and trusted God to provide the means. Parham rented a building dubbed "Stone's Folly". The owner had run out of money while building it. The ground floor was lavishly designed but the upstairs was poor by comparison. About forty students attended the first term. The only book permitted in this school was the Bible, and great emphasis was placed on corporate prayer. Apparently there was a Prayer Tower to which the students resorted for three-hour watches and sometimes nights of prayer. As soon as the students assembled they were given the task of discovering what was the biblical evidence of the Baptism in the Holy Spirit. Charles Parham had to leave for three days to speak at meetings in Kansas City, and when he returned he found the atmosphere in the college electric with excitement. They had all, on examining the New Testament, come to the conclusion that the answer to the question was "speaking in tongues as the Spirit gives utterance".

This was on the morning of the watchnight service, and the same evening the students, together with people from outside, met for this service. In Charles Parham's own words, "a mighty spiritual power filled the entire school".

They began to pray that they might be baptised in the Spirit as on the Day of Pentecost. As they were praying one of the students—Agnes Ozman—remembered that on three occasions in the New Testament hands had been laid on those desiring this blessing. So she asked Charles Parham if he would lay hands on her. At first he refused,

26

but then he agreed to do so. As he laid hands on her head "a glory fell upon her, a halo seemed to surround her head and face" and she began to speak in tongues. It was 7 p.m. on December 31st, 1900.

A number more, including Charles Parham himself, had similar experiences at the Topeka Bible School, but these early pioneers were largely given the cold shoulder by their friends and neighbours. There were a few further outbreaks in other centres, but by 1906 there were only about a thousand who had received the blessing in the entire United States.

In 1904 another significant event took place. Revival broke out in Wales. For a number of years Christians all over the world had been praying for a new spiritual awakening. The news about the amazing things which were happening in Tonypandy and other Welsh centres was flashed around the world and encouraged Christians to pray all the more fervently. If God had blessed Wales, they thought, why could not the same thing happen in their own countries?

One of those who had been praying for Los Angeles was Frank Bartleman, whose diary is about the best documentary evidence we have of the Azusa Street awakening. In April 1905 he heard F. B. Meyer speak in Los Angeles about the Welsh revival. "My soul was stirred to its depths," he wrote, "and I then and there promised God He should have full right of way with me, if He could use me." Next month he gave up all secular employment— "The Spirit of revival consumed me," he said. He wrote to Evan Roberts, the young Welsh revival leader, asking him to pray for California. He received a reply from Evan Roberts encouraging them to "Pray and wait. Believe God's promises."

The following year Frank Bartleman met an ordained Negro called W. J. Seymour. He had been a student at another Bible school which Charles Parham had opened at Houston, Texas, but had not been baptised in the Spirit. He had come to Los Angeles to preach at a small Negro church, but when they discovered that he believed in a Baptism in the Spirit with speaking in tongues they shut

27

their doors on him. This humble Negro was to be God's instrument in the work which was shortly to begin at Azusa Street. Finding the doors shut in his face, W. J. Seymour began to hold meetings at 214 North Bonnie Brae Street, and people experienced the Baptism in the Spirit. Their meeting place became increasingly unsuitable—for one thing the neighbours complained of the noise—so they moved to rented accommodation at 312 Azusa Street, an old livery stable, cum Methodist Church, cum lumber yard.

It was in this simple building that a sect became an international movement which was to circle the globe and fifty years later penetrate the sophisticated circles of the Episcopal and other churches.

The building had apparently long been disused for meetings and utilised for storing old lumber and plaster. When W. J. Seymour and his few friends arrived they cleared a space in the dirt and débris and laid some planks on the top of empty nail kegs—enough to seat about thirty people. Seymour was the leader, but like Evan Roberts in Wales he left most of the leading to the Holy Spirit. Someone described him as "dirty and collarless". His appearance must have been made still worse because he had only one eye. He generally sat behind two empty shoe boxes, one on top of the other, keeping his head inside the top one during the meetings.

"It had to start in poor surroundings to keep out the selfish human element," wrote Frank Bartleman. Those who came avoided human contact and greeting, but came to meet with God. The shekinah glory rested in this strange building. Some presumptuous men came to see what was going on, and tried to preach. They often finished up flat on their faces on the floor, "dying out", as Frank Bartleman picturesquely called it.

The Azusa Street revival lasted for about three years. People came from all over the world to witness what was going on. Meetings continued through the night as hundreds came to receive the blessing of the Baptism in the Spirit. Many more wrote to learn about what was going on. One of these was a Norwegian Methodist minister. But his story belongs to the next chapter.

CHAPTER THREE

IN SEARCH OF GOLD

In the autumn of 1905 a tall good-looking man disembarked in New York. His name was Thomas Ball Barratt. He was a well-known Methodist minister in Oslo, head of the City Mission. His purpose in coming to New York was to secure money to build a hall in the centre of Oslo. The United States was even then the happy hunting ground for fund-raising beggars. His mission was almost a complete failure, but he took back something of far greater value, which was to revolutionise not only his own life but many thousands of others. For it was in New York that he received the Baptism in the Spirit. Like the beggar at the beautiful gate of the Temple, healed by St. Peter, he came asking for money but left leaping for joy.

T. B. Barratt was born on July 22nd, 1862, at Albaston in Cornwall, near the Devonshire border. His parents were strict Wesleyans and his father a mining engineer. Shortly after he was born his father was offered the post of manager of a sulphur ore mine in Norway, which he accepted, and the whole family moved to their new home on the beautiful Hardanger Fjord. Later they sent their son Thomas to England for his education. He attended Queen's College in Taunton.

He was a born fighter and controversialist. He probably inherited this from his grandfather, Captain George Ball, who was a prominent local Methodist preacher in Cornwall. On one famous occasion the denominations challenged the local unitarians to a public debate, and they chose Captain Ball as their champion. While at school Thomas displayed gifts of leadership and musical talent. He was later to study for a time under Edward Greig and wrote a considerable amount of music as well as editing hymn-books. He seems to have been a deeply emotional person from an early age, and found in Methodism an outlet for his spiritual enthusiasm. Methodism was strong in Norway, but persecuted at times, especially by the Lutheran Church. He knew about religious controversy from an early age and soon entered the fray himself with vigour. At the age of twenty-one, for instance, we find him answering with his pen an attack on Methodism.

From his call to the ministry he seems to have worked extremely hard, on more than one occasion suffering physical breakdown through overwork. His desire for deeper experiences of God continued throughout the early period of his life. In 1888 he wrote in his diary, "Lord, baptise me fully in the Holy Ghost and fire." He was fearless in denouncing publicly the theatres then opening in Oslo. In 1902 he started work for the Central Mission in Oslo. Three years later he was in correspondence with Evan Roberts concerning the revival in Wales, asking for their prayer for Norway: "I want," he wrote, "a fuller baptism of fire." A few months later he left Norway for the United States, where God gave him what he asked for.

His visit to America seemed doomed to failure from the start. The day after he arrived he had a letter from his wife to say that his mother had died just after he had left Norway. He felt this loss keenly. The meetings were comparatively unsuccessful; no one seemed particularly interested in the Oslo City Mission and few wanted to give anything for the work. A terrible fire had ravaged San Francisco and most people seemed to want to give their money to the many homeless and bereaved. T. B. Barratt would have gone home if his bishop in Norway had not urged him to stay longer. He was advised, "Don't wait for something to turn up—turn up something." "There was a lot in that thought," he commented; "in fact it had been the red thread in my life, but perhaps I had made the mistake that I had often been turning up things in my own power—and the time was at hand when the Lord would teach me that He wanted to say more about my plans—yea—that He had a special plan for me, that was still hidden from view." It was soon to be revealed.

He stayed most of the time in Dr. A. B. Simpson's

Missionary Home in New York. He read the life of Charles Finney and was greatly impressed. But still the money did not come in. On September 11th, 1906, in a fit of depression, he wrote in his diary, "Numerous ways have been tried, but the results hitherto have been enough to knock down the courage of the most hopeful man that is to be found—where he is I do not know. ..." Later in his autobiography he wrote, "All the trials I had passed through during the last year in America brought me down, deeper down before the Lord, seeking, praying, weeping. ..."

About this time he heard about the revival which was taking place at Azusa Street in Los Angeles. He wrote an article about it in the Norwegian magazine which he edited, *Byposten*, which appeared in November 1906. By that time T. B. Barratt himself had experienced the Baptism in the Spirit, and his testimony was to appear in *Byposten* two issues later.

He never visited Los Angeles, but was in close correspondence with Azusa Street. He heard from a Mrs. May Throop, who urged him to seek this blessing: "We are praying the full pentecostal baptism upon you so that you may be equipped for His service as you never have been. ..."

On Sunday, October 7th, he attended a Communion service in Dr. Simpson's Home. It was taken by an Episcopal minister who had been converted through the Salvation Army. The organist was a Salvation Army girl in uniform. Several other ministers were present. Behind the altar on the wall stood the inscription—"*Jesus only*". After the service T. B. Barratt went upstairs to his room, locked the door and remained there all day fasting and praying. Shortly before 5 p.m. "the fire fell". He had to hide his face in a towel so as not to disturb his neighbours, as he shouted aloud his praises. "I was seized by the Holy Power of God throughout my whole being and it swept through my whole body as well ..." was how he afterwards described it. Next day he wrote in his diary, "I am the happiest man in the world, everything has become new, I am filled with peace and joy and love to God and man." Someone told him he looked ten years younger.

31

But he did not speak in tongues. He did not at the time expect tongues as a definite sign of the blessing, so he wrote to his friends in Los Angeles about this. They urged him to press on to receive the gift of tongues also. "The speaking in tongues," they wrote, "should follow the baptism. If you had remained under the power until the Lord had finished, you undoubtedly would have spoken in tongues. . . . Some go several days after the baptism before speaking. . . ."

On November 16th T. B. Barratt received what he now longed for—the gift of tongues—and with it a further deep experience of the Holy Spirit, so that later he doubted whether his October experience had in fact been the Baptism in the Spirit. On this occasion he was attending a meeting and hands were laid on him by a Norwegian Christian who happened to be there. While he was being prayed for someone saw a crown of fire over his head and a cloven tongue as of fire in front of the crown. He was immediately, in his own words, "filled with an indescribable power, and began to speak in a foreign language as loudly as I could . . . I am sure that I spoke seven or eight different languages—they were clear and plain." He also began to sing in the Spirit, and so continued until about 4 o'clock the next morning. He spoke, too, of "waves of God's love" sweeping over him, and of the spirit of supplication being given to him.

On December 8th he embarked on the *Campania* and sailed back to Norway. He was to meet a stormy reception. There was much criticism and conflict ahead, which ultimately led him and others reluctantly to resign from their churches and form a Pentecostal Church in Oslo. But this was not until 1916.

The years 1907–8 were golden ones for T. B. Barratt. Early in 1907 his story appeared in *Byposten* and the first sixteen Norwegians received the experience. The news spread quickly across Europe and there was great excitement in the Barratts' home as letters arrived from many countries asking for information and inviting him to speak at meetings. In January of that year a young Baptist minister in Sweden read Barratt's story in a Stockholm newspaper. He told a friend, "I'm going to Oslo tomorrow," and added; "I'm not coming back unless the Lord baptises me in the Holy Spirit." He was pastor of a small church in Lindköping and his name was Lewi Pethrus. He was soon back in Sweden. Barratt led him into the Baptism in the Spirit and they became firm friends. At this time Lewi Pethrus was only twenty-two, but he was to become one of the greatest Pentecostal leaders. In 1913, together with his church members, he was excluded from the Swedish Baptist Convention because he was practising open Communion. Today his church in Stockholm is the largest in Scandinavia, seating 4,000 persons. According to Nils Bloch-Hoell, "He represents the most sober form of Pentecostalism." Pethrus has written, "I joined entirely in the revival, but I considered it to be my task, for the blessing of God's work, to subdue its often fierce manifestations."[2]

In March 1907 a well-known German evangelist called to meet Barratt and see what God was doing. He was the Rev. Jonathan Paul, who had heard about the revival and wanted to find out for himself if it really was a work of God's Spirit. He became convinced, and shortly after returning to Germany received the experience he was seeking. Jonathan Paul, Donald Gee tells us in his history of the Pentecostal Movement, was a great holiness preacher and was called "the unsurpassed exponent of perfect love." He was also a very successful evangelist. Over 2,000 people were converted through a campaign he had held about this time in the Ruhr. He became a prominent leader of the movement in Germany.

In the same year an English tea planter in India, called A. N. Groves, heard of the Azusa Street revival from a couple who came from Los Angeles and were passing through India on their way to China as missionaries. That same year there had been a remarkable movement of the Spirit at Mukti through the ministry of the well-known Indian Christian, Pandita Ramabai. During this revival illiterate Indian girls prayed in English, a language which they had never learnt. Even in 1906 there were reports

33

coming from Auranzabad of speaking in tongues in work being carried on by the Church Missionary Society.

In spite of the opposition from some quarters to these events, A. N. Groves wrote to Barratt on January 8th, 1908, inviting him to India to speak to missionaries resting in the hill stations during the summer months. A cable was sent back accepting the invitation. Barratt spent three weeks in Bombay before moving on to Coonoor where Groves had arranged drawing-room meetings. There Barratt met an old Indian who had experienced the blessing eleven years before. He had been persecuted by Christians for speaking in tongues but continued to do so privately. "When I am very happy in the Lord and pray to Him, then it comes quite naturally," he told Barratt.

In August he returned to Europe. He stopped for a time in Denmark, where he received an invitation from the famous actress Anna Larssen, who had heard about the revival and became interested. Her drawing-room was packed with stage celebrities and reporters, but Barratt seemed to take it all in his stride. The press were sarcastic, but Anna Larssen herself was converted and later experienced the Baptism in the Spirit. She left the theatre and in 1912 married Sigurd Björner, the Y.M.C.A. secretary in Copenhagen. Together they organised the Danish Pentecostal Movement.

Barratt and most of those affected in these early days remained in their churches for a number of years, but a rift began to develop which grew wider and wider. In 1916, ten years after his initial experience, he resigned from the Methodist Church and organised the Filadelfia Church in Oslo. By 1926 Barratt had to write that it was impossible at that time to be a Pentecostal believer and at the same time remain a member of another denomination.

He was Pastor of the Filadelfia Church until his death in January 1940. He wrote over sixty books and pamphlets and played a vital part in the development of the Pentecostal Movement in Europe. He has rightly been called the apostle of Pentecostalism in Northern Europe. Alexander Boddy, the vicar of All Saints', Sunderland, described him as "manly, peaceful, rejoicing in the Lord, humble, yet strong for God". His great weakness was his fighting spirit. He often gave way to the temptation to hit back when under pressure of harsh criticism. During his visit to India an article was circularised to missionaries describing him as "Satan among the saints". His answer was addressed to "Satan among the critics". On one occasion he confessed, "I have at times allowed my strong feelings of justice to carry me too far in my judgement of others."

When the time came for Barratt to sever his last links with the Methodist Church, he sadly said goodbye to his many friends in that church. One of the last to shake him by the hand was Bishop W. Burt, who had encouraged him to go to the United States. As he grasped Barratt's hand he said affectionately, "Come back." He never did.

CHAPTER FOUR

A DEBT CONSUMED

"I WONDER if His Grace the Archbishop of Canterbury has heard of the Rev. Alexander A. Boddy?" wrote the reporter of the *Daily Chronicle* on October 13th, 1907.

He was writing about "strange things" in Monkwearmouth, Sunderland.

"Does he ever, I wonder," the report continued, "mount the watch-tower of his episcopal stronghold at Lambeth and peer out towards the North?"

It is extremely unlikely that Randall Davidson was "peering" at Sunderland at this precise moment. He was deeply involved in the controversy over the Education Bill, which Prime Minister Campbell-Bannerman had introduced in the Commons, and with preparing for the Pan-Anglican Congress and the Fifth Lambeth Conference due to be held the following year. He would have been far too engrossed with these matters to be concerned with the freak activities of Alexander Boddy.

Apart from the reporting of the newspapers it was even less likely that the general public would have heard of "yon queer chap" at Monkwearmouth—"the faith healer", as the locals called him.

Alexander Boddy had gone to All Saints', Sunderland, as a curate in 1884. He became vicar two years later and remained there until 1922, when he went to Piddington until his death. Before ordination in 1880 he had been a solicitor, and had also written travel books. While in Sunderland he became a Fellow of the Royal Geographical Society. He became an enthusiastic supporter of the Keswick Convention, a movement for the deepening of the spiritual life, which had been founded towards the end of the nineteenth century. In 1895 he published his only religious book, significantly called *The Laying-on of Hands*.

The Welsh revival of 1904–5 had a marked influence on

Mr. Boddy—as it had upon the Azusa Street meetings in America and T. B. Barratt in Norway. With many others he visited the revival centres in Wales and met the young leader of the revival—Evan Roberts.

Not long afterwards he heard about Barratt and what was happening in Norway. He was anxious to see for himself, so at the beginning of March 1907 he crossed the North Sea and met the Norwegian Methodist minister who was so much in the news at that time. He was deeply impressed. When he returned he wrote in several English newspapers: "My four days in Oslo can never be forgotten. I stood with Evan Roberts in Tonypandy, but have never witnessed such scenes as those in Norway."

He went to Keswick for the Convention later that year and enthusiastically distributed thousands of copies of a tract he had written called *Pentecost for England*. He met with a very cool reception and few seemed to share his zeal.

Throughout 1907 the religious press seemed to censor all news about the Pentecostal revival. Apart from one favourable article in *The Christian* by a Dr. Mercer, there was stony silence. Many eyes were watching—some mouths were whispering—but no one was shouting the news from the rooftops.

First into battle seems to have been an organisation ironically called "the Pentecostal Mission". They had been founded in 1888 by Reader Harris and produced a magazine called *Tongues of Fire*. They were campaigning against the formality of much religious life and were concerned with spreading "scriptural holiness". Strangely enough, part of their teaching included "the Baptism of the Holy Ghost as a definite blessing received after conversion".

The news of the Pentecostal revival touched this organisation on the raw. In April 1907 an article appeared which was most critical of "speaking in tongues". Later another one was included, which had been written by Oswald Chambers, attacking "spiritual ecstasy tongues". Then came the meetings in Sunderland, which we shall be describing in a moment. They provoked a storm of abuse.

In November there was an article describing the gift of tongues as "a satanic counterfeit". T. B. Barratt, though not mentioned by name, is described as being of the "people from America and from other parts of the world" sent by the devil. But by January 1908 they had had to admit that they had suffered much from "this strange movement with its deplorable accompaniments".

Meanwhile Alexander Boddy was not discouraged by all this and started to badger T. B. Barratt to visit his church for meetings. On Saturday August 31st, 1907, the Norwegian Methodist leader disembarked at Newcastle and was met by his excited friend.

No time apparently was lost, and the same evening a prayer meeting was held in the vestry of the church. The next day Barratt preached in the church at the evening service. There was an after meeting which continued in a very un-Anglican fashion until 4 a.m., and the first three members of All Saints' were filled with the Holy Spirit as on the Day of Pentecost, "speaking in other tongues as the Spirit gave them utterance".

The news spread far and wide—helped by the national press which could not resist the temptation of such sensational headlines as "STRANGE REVIVALIST SCENES—VICAR'S CHILD TALKS CHINESE." Another reporter told the story of "staid unemotional matrons taken home to bed o' night 'drunk' with ecstatic joy". No doubt the reporters would have written the same about the scene at Pentecost when "some mocked and others said, 'these men are full of new wine'".

T. B. Barratt stayed until the middle of October and was apparently kept very busy all through these seven weeks. The meetings were held in the large vestry of All Saints' church. They were comparatively quiet and orderly and there was no working up of people's emotions. Some who came from the Salvation Army found them a little "flat" compared with their own gatherings. Occasionally Mr. Boddy held an all night "waiting meeting". Mrs. Boddy received the experience before her husband, and was very active in counselling people. It was she who opened the door to the plumber from Bradford, Smith Wigglesworth, later to become a well-known and much loved Pentecostal leader. It was she who talked to him, prayed with him and led him into the experience.

Just as Azusa Street had been used in America, so now this staid Anglican church became the mecca for pilgrims seeking the experience of God's Spirit. They travelled up from London and the south coast—from Yorkshire and Wales and many did not return disappointed.

"Oh, those transformed faces ... the joy of some has been inexpressible," wrote Barratt in his diary.

He taught them a hymn which he had written in America, "I have reached the sunny hilltops of Zion", and wrote several tracts which Mr. Boddy widely circulated. Invitations poured in for him to speak at other centres in Britain, but he had to return to Norway. In the farewell meetings they all joined hands and prayed and sang together. The vicar thanked him for "honouring the Blood and honouring the Bible". A wildly excited crowd saw him off at Sunderland station, and at Newcastle the vicar and a few others saw him on to the boat.

Whether or not the Primate of All England was "gazing from the watch-tower" we do not know—but we do know that nearer the scene of these events there was an ecclesiastical dignitary who was keenly interested. Dr. Handley Moule, the Bishop of Durham, had been an early opponent of the Keswick Convention and had regarded it as dangerously subjective in its teaching. Later he was humble enough to alter his views and supported the Convention wholeheartedly for the rest of his life. He was to be a frequent speaker on the Keswick platform. Bishop Moule had experienced a revival when a young minister and had rejoiced to see the power of God moving in an unusual fashion. It was strangely fortuitous for Alexander Boddy that he should have had such a sympathetic bishop, for he raised no objections to the meetings which were to continue at Sunderland for some time to come.

There was another strange coincidence. Not far from All Saints' there was a well-known Baptist church called Bethesda. The minister was an up-and-coming speaker and Bible teacher. His name was Graham Scroggie. He was later to become one of the best-known of Keswick speakers. Before he came to Sunderland he had been turned out of two churches because of his opposition to modernism and worldliness. But now he was to become one of the main opponents of the Pentecostal Movement.

Mr. Boddy did not lack support in other directions. Mail poured into the Sunderland vicarage, forcing him to engage two full-time secretaries. The following year it was decided to hold a Whitsun Convention at Sunderland. It was to be the first of many such gatherings. Alexander Boddy sent out the invitations and admission was by ticket only. Only those in full sympathy were allowed to the meetings and strict rules were enforced to ensure that everything was done in an orderly fashion. The text above the platform was "fervent in Spirit". About the same time Mr. Boddy published a magazine called *Confidence*, which though intended for this country was rapidly circulated all over the world.

If a cultured Anglican parson and writer of travel books seems rather out of place in this story, so too does the squire of Howbury Hall.

Cecil Polhill had inherited Howbury Hall in 1903. It was an eighteenth century country house near Bedford with extensive grounds. He was to live there until his death in 1938. He was educated at Eton and Cambridge. On going down from the university he went into the army. It was while he was serving in the army that his younger brother Arthur was converted in the famous Moody Mission at Cambridge. Cecil heard all about it from Arthur, and was shocked to hear that his brother was thinking of going to China as a missionary.

But in 1884 Cecil too was converted, and then became linked with C. T. Studd. Together with his brother Arthur he became a member of the famous Cambridge Seven. They left for China in 1885.

Cecil and his wife worked for most of the time on the Tibetan border. They nearly lost their lives in a riot in 1892. He was described by someone as "quiet and dogged".

40

He received the Baptism in the Spirit at a drawing-room meeting while he was in Los Angeles on a visit to the United States. When he returned to England he soon got into touch with Alexander Boddy and linked up with him in the work which was opening up at that time. He never left the Anglican Church, but continued to support the Pentecostal Movement throughout his life. He also served during this time on the Council of the China Inland Mission.

Up to the outbreak of the First World War Alexander Boddy and Cecil Polhill continued to exercise strong influence and leadership. But the war saw the initiative moving in another direction. By 1918 Mr. Boddy was a shadow of his former self. Although he continued to be vicar of All Saints' until 1922 he was to play no further active part in the development of the movement. By the end of the war the main Pentecostal groups had been or were in the process of being formed. The movement was becoming a denomination and the churches had virtually turned their backs on it. The Anglican and Free Churches had barely been touched.

So Alexander Boddy slipped into obscurity, while men like Smith Wigglesworth, Stanley Frodsham (later to write Wigglesworth's biography) and others, who had been led into blessing by him, came more into the limelight. Like Cecil Polhill he never left the Anglican Church. He was a prophet few listened to, and most forgot. But an inscription on the wall of his church hall reminds us how a church debt was consumed when the fire fell at All Saints', Sunderland:

September 1907

WHEN

THE FIRE OF THE LORD

FELL

IT BURNED UP THE DEBT

CHAPTER FIVE

"THAT'S NOT MY SMITH"

A BRADFORD plumber was speaking and the audience was gripped. His wife Polly normally did all the talking, but this time she was sitting critically at the back. She was an ardent Salvationist. "This will teach him a lesson," she had said to herself, "claiming to be more baptised in the Spirit than me, and speaking in tongues and all." She'd be there to see him make a fool of himself. That would soon knock some sense into him.

He spoke from the text that Jesus read when He returned to His home church after His experience of power at the River Jordan. "The Spirit of the Lord God is upon me because the Lord has anointed me...." The eyes of that critical audience were riveted on Jesus, and now the same thing was happening in that Bradford chapel. He usually sat meekly beside his wife while she harangued the people in her dynamic way, but now he was on his feet facing at least one strong critic. Polly became more and more agitated as he went on, until unable to contain herself any longer she cried out in a voice that many could hear: "That's not my Smith, Lord, that's not my Smith."

Smith Wigglesworth had just returned from the vicarage in Sunderland, having received what he had gone for—the Baptism in the Spirit and speaking in tongues. His wife was indignant, but now she knew that "her Smith" was not the same man he had been before. That night she witnessed the beginning of a ministry which was to take her husband around the world. She was not by any means the only person to notice the difference, for when Wigglesworth had finished speaking and sat down, the secretary of the mission sprang to his feet and said, "I want what our leader has received."

The Pentecostal Movement in Britain was to be shaped by plumbers and miners rather than by parsons and country squires. Down in Maesteg, waiting to be rocketed to fame, lived the Jeffreys brothers. Stephen was a miner and George worked in the Co-op. They were shortly to receive their Pentecost, and were later to make an important contribution to the growth of the movement.

In 1859 the famous Irish revival broke out in Ulster. It was in that year too that William Booth left the Methodist Church and went to work in London's East End. He was later to found the Salvation Army. But it was also the year that Smith Wigglesworth was born. It was as if fate desired to underline his obscurity and lowliness of birth that he was named as he was. His birthplace was a broken-down shack in Menston, Yorkshire. His father was a pauper and Smith began work at the age of six, pulling up and cleaning turnips. A year later he went to work in a woollen mill.

He was brought up as an Anglican and taken to the bishop for confirmation. As the bishop laid his hands on him, "I had a similar experience to the one I had fourteen years later when I was baptised in the Spirit," he told people years later. "My whole body was filled with the consciousness of God's presence, a consciousness that remained with me for days. After the confirmation service all the other boys were swearing and quarrelling, and I wondered what had made the difference between them and me."

When his family moved to Bradford he joined the Methodist Church there, disliking the formalism of the Established Church. He was then thirteen years old. But even the Methodists did not seem to possess the fire he wanted, so three years later he joined a newly opened branch of the Salvation Army.

Smith Wigglesworth must have been typical of many others who were dissatisfied with the tedious formality of much organised religion in this country at the beginning of this century, and who were to become the backbone of the Salvation Army and later the Pentecostals. It is not fair always to attribute selfish motives to spiritual vagrancy. If people want "fire" and enthusiasm and don't receive it in their own churches, they will be tempted to look for it somewhere else. This enthusiasm is as much part of the genuine Christian tradition as forms of services, and Smith Wigglesworth was only one of many who preferred living sectarianism to dead catholicity.

Wigglesworth had already begun his healing ministry before he went to Sunderland to receive his baptism in the Holy Spirit. He had experienced a most remarkable healing from peritonitis. The doctor who examined him held out very little hope apart from an operation, and he reckoned he was too weak to survive it. An elderly woman and a young man who believed in the power of God to heal visited him just after the doctor had gone and prayed for his healing. The result was dramatic.

"To my surprise," he said, "I felt as well as I had ever been in my life. I was absolutely free from pain. As soon as they had prayed for me they went downstairs and I got up."

He went out immediately to do a plumbing job, to the consternation of the doctor when he returned a little later. "They will bring back a corpse, as sure as you live," said the doctor.

Telling the story years later Wigglesworth added: "The 'corpse' has been going up and down the world preaching the gospel these many years since that time."

Smith Wigglesworth's healing campaigns always drew crowds. He maintained his simplicity to the end of a long and distinguished life. Like his Master he wrote no books. He never read anything but the Bible.

But Pentecostalism did not make the same impact upon Britain as it did upon other countries, particularly Scandinavia and North and South America. In Norway and Sweden it is the strongest non-Catholic denomination. In the United States it ranks seventh in size with nearly two million members. In some South American countries there has been phenomenal growth, particularly in Brazil and Chile. To give some idea of the following the Pentecostal Church in Chile has: recently when Manuel Umaña, one of their founder members, died, his funeral was attended by 100,000 people. He had been pastor of a church for fifty-five years and seen its membership grow to 15,000. In the

Chilean parliament political leaders paid their respects to this Christian leader. According to Canon Douglas Webster the Pentecostal churches are today growing faster in these two countries "than any other church anywhere and possibly faster than any other church at any other period of history".[3] In Chile there are a million Pentecostals out of a population of 7½ million. In one part of Brazil, Canon Webster reports, one Pentecostal church has 227 congregations after nine years' work. One of these groups is building a temple in São Paolo to hold 25,000 people; "without doubt that temple will often be full". But these figures appear even more revealing when studied in terms of growth. In Chile, for instance, the church membership in 1932 was only 10,000—showing a hundredfold increase in just over thirty years. In the United States the membership of one Pentecostal denomination rose from 50,386 in 1925 to 514,317 in 1962. In the same period the number of ordained ministers increased from barely a thousand to nearly ten thousand. When most other churches in the same period have tended to decline, or at the most barely hold their own, this is a significant and remarkable achievement.

But why has not the same thing happened in Britain? The movement certainly suffered early on from uncertain leadership. To begin with Alexander Boddy and Cecil Polhill exercised a wise restraint on over-zealous propagation of Pentecostalism. They were determined to keep the movement in the churches—while the churches seemed equally determined to keep it out. There was no one with the skill of Barratt or Pethrus to lead the movement in its early stages. When leaders came to the front, they did not command the respect at first that the Scandinavian pioneers obviously did. "There can be no doubt," writes Donald Gee in his book *The Pentecostal Movement*, "that for many precious years the movement floundered for lack of strong, inspiring, distinctive leadership such as might have welded it into a mighty spiritual force in the land."[4]

Both Barratt and Pethrus were convinced from the start of the need for church discipline, with their strong

45

Methodist and Baptist backgrounds. In Chile, too, practically the whole Methodist Episcopal Church seceded and became Pentecostal, but their theology and church government remained Methodist, including the continuance of infant baptism. But men like Smith Wigglesworth, George and Stephen Jeffreys and so on had little or no theological background.

The two world wars also hindered the growth of the movement in this country. Scandinavia, North and South America were mostly unaffected by the First World War, and for the most part less affected than Britain by the Second World War. In the First World War many of the Pentecostals became conscientious objectors, which did not make them too popular. Both Alexander Boddy and Cecil Polhill were patriots at heart and warmly supported the war effort, which did not encourage the deepening rift between them and the others.

Then in the face of this weakness, especially when it came to apologetics—for the movement came under heavy fire from the moment of its birth in this country—there was immensely strong opposition from Christian leaders. Donald Gee writes, "Many were frightened from even making a personal contact and enquiry for themselves. Only at the cost of great reproach could believers join themselves to any of the despised little Pentecostal meetings."[5] Men like F. B. Meyer, A. T. Pierson and Oswald Chambers were against the movement, Nils Bloch-Hoell tells us. So was Graham Scroggie, as we have already seen. But the movement met mostly indifference and ridicule. "Some mocked and others said, 'We will hear you again on this matter'"—but they never did. A story is told of Smith Wigglesworth attending some Christian gathering where none of the speakers seemed to get to the point. So Wigglesworth, taking his jacket off, strode to the front and fired off some good Pentecostal broadsides. Although we can admire his courage, his method was not likely to commend itself to the intractable antagonists of the Pentecostal experience. But we must understand the feelings of men who suffered the most terrible reproach and ridicule from their Christian brethren. Many of them were expelled from their churches and branded as "agents of the devil". Some of them "gave as good as they got", but it did not help to commend the message.

One of the main reasons for the formation of the Pentecostal churches in this country was the protection of the movement from what Donald Gee calls "worthless religious tramps".[6] He goes on to say, "The amazing freedom of the meetings gave opportunity for undesirables to take advantage for personal ends." This was a real stumbling block also to the many observers, who invariably saw the excesses and reared away in horror. This all gave encouragement to false stories and exaggerated accounts which gave many a false picture of what really was going on. Many never even bothered to look to see what it was all about, so garbled were the accounts that reached their ears.

So the movement ceased to care whether it was accepted or not. Between the wars there was immense and, by most standards, very successful evangelism, largely through the labours of the Jeffreys brothers. It maintained polite relations with the other churches, but each wanted the other to know there was a fence between and it was best to keep at a safe distance from each other.

But a second breath of Pentecostal wind was on its way —and both parties now are becoming less sure about that fence and less suspicious of their neighbours.

PART TWO

SECOND WIND

CHAPTER SIX

A FORECAST COMES TRUE

A YOUNG man sat behind his office desk. He was an early riser and liked to spend the early hours of the morning working. His name was David du Plessis and he was then General Secretary of the Apostolic Faith Mission of South Africa. It was 1936, and he had the inimitable Smith Wigglesworth staying with him. It was about 7 a.m.

Suddenly the door flew open and in walked Smith Wigglesworth. He commanded the startled du Plessis to come out from behind the desk. Laying his hands on his shoulders he pushed him against the wall and began to prophesy: "You have been in 'Jerusalem' long enough.... I will send you to the uttermost parts of the earth.... You will bring the message of Pentecost to all churches.... You will travel more than most evangelists do.... God is going to revive the churches in the last days and through them turn the world upside down...."

Then he began to tell him details of visions he had been seeing that morning and which God had told him to share. It was all too fantastic. Even the Pentecostal Movement would become a mere joke compared with the revival which God was bringing through the churches. He wished he were younger to see these things, but God had revealed that they would come to pass after he had died. God would require two things of his servant—faithfulness and humility. Great things would come to pass through his ministry, du Plessis was told, and he would play an important part in this coming revival in the churches.

Then Wigglesworth went out as quickly as he had come, leaving a dumbfounded young man to ruminate on this strange prophecy. He could then see no possibility of its fulfilment. It was impossible, Wigglesworth must have been mistaken. Were not the historic churches, together with the Roman Catholic Church, the Beast and Scarlet

Woman of Revelation, doomed to the lake of fire? Were not these churches hopelessly corrupted by formalism and modernistic teaching? How could God do anything with such deadness? Had he not consistently counselled people to leave these churches—to "come out from among them"?

And what about his own life? He had never travelled outside his own native South Africa. He was safely entrenched in an interesting and rewarding job. How was he going to become a globe-trotter? These and other thoughts were going through his mind when there was another loud knock on the door of his office.

It was the beaming Smith Wigglesworth again, though this time he greeted du Plessis with a friendly "Good morning" as if he had not seen him before that day. Du Plessis expressed his surprise.

"When God gives me a message," Smith Wigglesworth replied, "He tells me to greet no man on the way. That is what I did. Now I have delivered the message, I can greet you and speak to you. By the way, have you ever suffered from air or sea sickness?"

"No," said du Plessis, "I've never travelled by air or sea."

"Then come out from behind that desk," said Wigglesworth.

Once again hands were laid on his shoulders and Wigglesworth prayed that the young du Plessis would never suffer sickness in travel. He never has.

"You'll be beginning your travels soon," was Wigglesworth's final remark.

Within three weeks, quite out of the blue, came an invitation to attend the General Council of the Assemblies of God in the United States the following year.

Du Plessis was away for ten months. At the Bible School in Pasadena, California, he met Dr. Charles Price, a well-known Pentecostal evangelist, and shared with him the amazing prophecies made the year before in his office in South Africa. Dr. Price wept with joy when he heard the story, and thanked God that it confirmed what had been shown him about the future. He encouraged du Plessis to believe the prophecy and wait to see its fulfilment in due course. He was himself convinced that both Protestants and Roman Catholics would receive another great stirring by the Holy Spirit. Neither he nor Wigglesworth had any idea how all this would come to pass—they simply believed.

In 1939 the Second World War broke out and du Plessis, back in South Africa, had no further opportunities for travel. On March 12th, 1947, Smith Wigglesworth died, and the same year du Plessis began his travels, which, first with the Pentecostal Movement and then as a free-lance moving among the historic churches, were to take him all over the world. The prophecy was fulfilled to the letter. Between June and August 1960 he travelled over 12,000 miles, and he has become about the most travelled Christian leader in the world.

Then in the fifties—only a few years after Wigglesworth's death—the prophecy of revival in the churches began to come true. What had seemed impossible to the young man behind that office desk was actually taking place and, as prophesied, he was playing a significant part in it.

CHAPTER SEVEN

MR. PENTECOST

"I'LL be back by lunch-time," David du Plessis called out to his wife Anna as he left their Connecticut home. It was only a short journey in the train to the headquarters of the World Council of Churches in New York, and he didn't expect to get very far with that.

To Anna it had been quite a surprise when David asked for an early breakfast that morning and told her where he was going.

"What will you try next?" he remembered her saying.

"I'm not trying anything," said David, "I'm just obeying the Lord."

It was not far to the offices of the W.C.C. on Fifth Avenue, but David might have been trying to leap across the Niagara Falls for all that most people thought would come of it. It was the first direct attempt by anyone to bridge the chasm between the Protestants and Pentecostals. Most members of the World Council of Churches had hardly heard of the Pentecostals. Most Pentecostals regarded the W.C.C. with the gravest mistrust and suspicion.

David was travelling not on a hunch but in obedience to a call, which was to have far-reaching repercussions. He was later to be dubbed by a reporter "Mr. Pentecost" in recognition of his role as a mediator in three-cornered Christendom: for there are three not two main streams of Christian life and tradition—as Bishop Lesslie Newbigin has made clear in his book *Household of God*—the Catholic, the Protestant and the Pentecostal. So Mr. Pentecost went to town, and as it turned out never got back for that lunch his wife prepared.

David's life was a preparation for that trip to New York. He was born in South Africa in 1905, and there is French Huguenot blood in his veins. When he was nine his father went one evening into a derelict Presbyterian church in

Johannesburg to hear two Americans who had witnessed the Azusa Street revival telling all about it. It changed his father's life, and he offered his services as a carpenter to the new mission stations which were being built in the African hills. The whole family joined the Pentecostal Church and when he was thirteen David himself experienced the Baptism in the Spirit.

He grew up in the atmosphere of bitter conflict. His parents were turned out of the Dutch Reformed Church, and their young son did not easily forget the injustice of this action to parents he knew to be saints. He used to go and listen to the ministers preaching against the Pentecostals, and learned to hit back at "these blind leaders of the blind", as they called them.

From 1928, when he was ordained by the Apostolic Faith Mission of South Africa, until that trip in 1952, he remained firmly in his Pentecostal shell, having little or no contact with the "dry old churches", as he thought of them.

He gradually rose in South African Pentecostal circles, where he became editor of a newspaper, and in the international sphere until he was appointed Secretary of the Second Pentecostal World Conference in Paris in 1949. In that same year he left South Africa and settled with his family in the United States. Increasingly his heart was bent on uniting all the Pentecostal churches throughout the world into an international organisation—a scheme which some Pentecostals fervently opposed, particularly the Scandinavians. With all his skill and energy he tried to bring this about—without success. But God had a different plan for his life. It was shortly to be revealed. It lay in a new direction entirely, and God had to deal with the old du Plessis before it could begin.

It happened in the midst of a whirlwind of appointments preparing for the Paris Conference of 1949. Driving to an appointment in the hills of Tennessee his car hit a locomotive in dense fog on an unmanned crossing. David's head went through the windscreen and he received serious injuries. Rushed to hospital, it took him a long time before he was fit enough to resume work. When he did, he was a new person. The long period in hospital gave God a chance to change David into a different person for the ministry He had prepared for him. Gradually he came to realise that his future no longer lay in trying to get all Pentecostals to think alike. But where he was to go and what he was to do was not yet clear. He was soon to know.

As a Pentecostal David had regarded the W.C.C. with grave suspicion. But now he was discovering that God was telling him to go and witness to their leaders.

"But, Lord," he pleaded, "I have preached so much against them. What do I say to them now? They won't listen to me. Their churches have put our people out of their fellowship." But still the inner urge and insistence was maintained. So he ordered the early breakfast and caught the train to New York.

"I gave my name," he related later, "to the girl at the reception desk, and made sure there was no mistake about who and what I was. A Pentecostal, and one of the worst, actually the world secretary. On the train I had rehearsed what I was going to say, and I was going to make things so hot for those leaders that they were sure to reject me."

In his anxiety to obey he had not thought about making an appointment—but God had arranged all that for him. He saw a few men the first day, and more later. They listened and asked questions. The hotter David made it, the more they liked it—and the more they wanted to hear. They invited him out to lunch. They did the eating while David did the talking.

"Where have you been all this time?" they asked. "We have been waiting for someone like you to come and tell us about Pentecost."

David found his own attitude changing. Suddenly he discovered that he was no longer talking to stuffy old liberals, but to his own brothers. Another wall was coming down.

As a result of this encounter David was invited to his first ecumenical conference—the International Missionary Council at Willingen in Germany. He checked in for three days, reckoning this would be about the limit of his powers of endurance. But he stayed much longer. He arrived during a coffee break on the first day, and Dr. John A. Mackay took him by the arm and introduced him to many of the delegates as "my great Pentecostal friend". This broke the ice and opened the door. One man had obeyed God rather than his personal feelings, and as a result there opened up for him an international ministry of far-reaching consequences. In 1954 Dr. Visser 't Hooft, the Secretary of the W.C.C., invited David to attend the Second Assembly at Evanston as a member of the staff. It was the beginning of a remarkably successful invasion of ecumenical circles by David du Plessis.

When in 1956 he was invited to speak to twenty-four ecumenical leaders he described his experience in this way: "That morning something happened to me. After a few introductory words I suddenly felt a warm glow come over me. I knew this was the Holy Spirit taking over. But what was He doing to me? Instead of the harsh spirit of criticism and condemnation in my heart, I now felt such love and compassion for those ecclesiastical leaders that I would rather have died for them than pass sentence upon them. All at once I knew that the Holy Spirit was in control.... Thank God, from that day on I knew what it meant to minister along the 'more excellent way'. This indeed is the technique of the Holy Spirit."

When you meet or hear David du Plessis you know immediately the truth and sincerity of these words. You may disagree and dislike what he is saying, but you cannot object to the man who is saying it. He has not compromised his Pentecostal views one iota. He still believes that speaking in tongues is the scriptural consequence of the Baptism in the Holy Spirit. But he has been delivered from his Pentecostal prejudice and censoriousness, and this is one of the reasons why he is in such demand internationally as a speaker.

One illustration will bear this out. An Anglican priest, then a member of the Brotherhood of St. Francis, called Norman Scovell, had heard that his brother Gordon, who was an Episcopal priest working in California, had got mixed up with a group of fanatics, and was now speaking in tongues. This alarmed him so much that he arranged to see his brother in order to steer him gently back to the paths of orthodoxy. But he soon found himself with his brother attending a meeting at which David du Plessis was present.

He found du Plessis a very different person from the mental picture he had formed of Pentecostals. He discovered that he had an amazing insight and empathy regarding the nature and purpose of monasticism. David charitably omitted, for example, all references to the many unfortunate abuses performed by those who felt called to this life. Norman Scovell remembered a lot of that conversation: "He raised the subject concerning the use of Latin in the Roman Catholic liturgy and admitted that it would contribute greatly to clerical communication and lingual unification. This type of conversation I had thought improbable and impossible with one of his position. At no time did he succumb to opinionated discourse. However, he left me with the impression that he felt that apostolic succession of *power* was of greater importance than apostolic succession of *authority*.... He then went on to speak of the infilling of the Holy Spirit as an even greater means of unification than the use of Latin.... He commended the Anglican Church for her Book of Common Prayer, having examined it previously. I could see that this had been more than a cursory examination. Through his travels he had come to the conclusion that such a common liturgy frequently served to bind different branches of the Body into one communion."

This was typical of the approach of David du Plessis. Norman's prejudices melted away and he received the Baptism in the Spirit that same day. It is David's genuine love and warm humility which makes him such an able and successful ambassador for Christ.

His ministry has become increasingly costly, as he has lost face with some Pentecostals who cannot stomach his apparent wooing of liberal theologians and his more recent overtures to Roman Catholics.

"This is for me a faith venture," he has courageously said. "No one hires me and so no one can fire me. I have resigned from every position I held, and so I have become just a great 'has been'.... I travel as the Lord provides, and He takes care of my family too."

When criticised for his ecumenical activities he has replied: "The Holy Spirit has never recognised barriers. He goes to the synagogue as well as the heavenly temple. He moves upon Jews, Samaritans and Gentiles. He is *universal* in His operations and *ecumenical* in His outreach."

Another frequent criticism concerns the emotionalism of some meetings. His reply has been: "I would rather see people, any time, weep for sheer joy in the Holy Ghost, than to see them weeping in a theatre because of some 'make-believe' show. I fear we are so afraid of emotionalism that we have caused people to give expression to their feelings in amusement centres."

On one occasion he was present at a Presbyterian church meeting where the gifts of the Spirit were manifested very freely, one after the other. After the service the minister turned to David and said: "Do you realise—we've had all the gifts of the Spirit except the gift of miracles."

"Oh, yes, we have," retorted David, "the miracle is that all this was going on in a Presbyterian church."

And it all happened after someone had an argument with a locomotive at a railway crossing and the harsh spirit of a Pentecostal preacher was broken and mellowed.

CHAPTER EIGHT

ST. MARK'S PASSION

"IT was a lovely service, Father," said a sweet elderly lady as she left St. Mark's Episcopal church, Van Nuys, after the morning service on Passion Sunday, 1960.

This was what she always said, and through her eyes it had been like any other service on any other Sunday. In actual fact the service set off an earthquake whose tremors were picked up on ecclesiastical seismographs all over the world. The rector, the Rev. Dennis Bennett, had preached that morning and told the congregation that he had been filled with the Holy Spirit and had spoken with other tongues, just like the apostles and others on the Day of Pentecost. One of the curates had taken off his vestments, publicly resigned and walked out down the centre aisle of the church. At another service that day another curate had declared to the congregation that such things could not be tolerated in respectable churches. The church treasurer suggested to the rector after the service that he ought to resign, which he later agreed to do. "Women wept and strong men left the church with drawn brows," went one report, "but that same sweet elderly lady took the curate's hand and said, 'It was a lovely service, Father.'"

Bishop Bloy of Los Angeles heard about what had happened and issued a pastoral letter banning any more speaking in tongues under church auspices. In June the news hit the headlines and both *Time* and *Newsweek* wrote the story up. In July, Dennis Bennett left for another church. But it was not a storm in a teacup. What happened that Sunday morning in Van Nuys brought into the open a movement which had been gathering momentum in the United States and Canada for at least four years. It gave many other ministers and lay people courage to come out into the open and declare what God had been doing in their lives. There had been a growing concern for a return to the vital experience which New Testament Christians had possessed through the Holy Spirit. The events of that Passion Sunday caused this interest to spread and deepen in all the principal denominations of North America.

But how did Dennis Bennett—a successful Episcopal rector of a fashionable and go-ahead church—get involved in what some would call "the eccentricities of Pentecostalism"? It is an intriguing story.

It really began when a young Episcopal couple came into contact for the first time with Christians who had a deep experience and awareness of God. John and Joan Baker had been searching for reality for some time. A relative had left the Episcopal Church and joined the Mormons, but this did not seem to be the answer for them. Then one day their close friends, a dentist and his wife, experienced the Baptism in the Spirit. The difference in Chuck and Shirley was instant and impressive. They noticed the inward peace and calm they now possessed. So Joan asked Shirley what had happened to her—she answered in the heavenly language that the Lord had given her. Joan tells what her reaction to this was: "I was astonished—for the first time in my life I knew that God was real; that He was as near to me as Shirley. My first thought was, 'The New Testament is true. How wonderful that God still heals, performs miracles and speaks through His people.' Another realisation hit me—I was a sinner—then the Lord led me through a period of repentance."

A week after this first encounter with the power of the Holy Spirit Joan was similarly baptised in the Holy Spirit and spoke in other tongues, and so were her husband John and their young daughter Cathy.

When Sunday came round the question arose—Where shall we go? They had been nominal churchgoers, attending occasionally their local Episcopal church, but having no enthusiasm for its services or fellowship. Should they now go to the Pentecostals? They would at least be welcomed and understood. By the strangest coincidence their Episcopal church was named "the Church of the Holy Spirit", so they went back there and sat shyly in the back pew.

They talked to no one, and no one talked to them. Not a promising start.

They thought they ought to share their experience with their vicar, the Rev. Frank Maguire. He was completely nonplussed, but he had to admit that they were not the wild-eyed fanatics he had thought they would be. In fact they turned out to be better Episcopalians than most he knew. Without any prompting from him they threw themselves wholeheartedly into the work of the church, attending the weekly study class and the mid-week communion service. Later they began to tithe. So Frank thought the best thing to do would be to surround these nice people with the most balanced members of his church in the hope that they would "straighten out" and forget this strange deviation from Episcopal orthodoxy. But to his increasing consternation one by one these nice balanced church members of his began to get interested in the experience described by John and Joan. Within the next few months, in fact, though he did not know it then, a dozen or so members of the church were to be filled with the Spirit and to speak in tongues. The vicar confided afterwards that whenever he saw anyone talking with John and Joan he was sure that another Episcopalian was doomed.

So Frank decided to seek the help and advice of his friend Dennis Bennett, who was rector of a neighbouring church. He found Dennis if anything more ignorant than himself about the whole matter. He joked later: "I didn't know enough about speaking in tongues to be prejudiced against it."

But somehow there was a response and echo in these men which answered to this strange pastoral problem. They had both had a real conversion experience when young. Frank had been brought up in Northern Ireland and had accepted Christ as his Saviour at a C.S.S.M. beach mission. Dennis, who had been born in London, had also been converted when a child, but had been drawn into the arid desert of professionalism. He knew that he was good at explaining to people all *about* God, and the basic Christian doctrines, but his own experience of God Himself had become increasingly intellectual. To him it was like a clicking camera shutter—one moment God was there and then He wasn't. Moreover he found himself moving more and more in a sacramental direction in an attempt to satisfy the basic hunger of his heart; then he had become interested in divine healing and the liturgical movement. Dennis had been very successful at Van Nuys. His church roll now stood at 2,500 members. The services were packed and he seemed to have everything he could possibly want, and yet he was not satisfied. Somehow, good though it all seemed on paper, it was not the kind of church he read about in the New Testament.

This encounter with John and Joan Baker did something for Dennis and Frank. In November 1959 Dennis entered into the experience of being filled with the Holy Spirit when John prayed with him, and spoke in other tongues. Frank followed three days later with the same experience. For both of them there was an immediate change. They found themselves witnessing with a new freedom and success. Many of the sick they had previously only prayed for, were now healed by the power of God. They had an intense love for the Lord Jesus Christ and their fellow Christians, and Dennis lost all interest in time-consuming hobbies.

Dennis Bennett began to send members of his congregation who were interested to John and Joan, and during the following four months eight ministers and nearly a hundred laymen from the diocese were baptised in the Holy Spirit. Among these were some of the key members of St. Mark's church, Van Nuys, including the junior warden, the directress of the altar guild, the choirmaster and members of the other organisations. By April 3rd, 1960, some seventy members of the church had experienced the Holy Spirit in this way.

They tried to keep quiet about it, but the news inevitably leaked out. It may be true that young children should be "seen and not heard", but this axiom certainly does not fit Christianity. When the early Christians were told to keep quiet, they politely but firmly told the authorities that it was impossible for them to be silent about what they had seen and heard. So in Van Nuys too the news got around

63

and the usual ugly rumours went with it. Dissension and misunderstanding arose. Fantastic allegations were spread. It was seriously believed by some that there were members of the church rolling on the ground under the power of the Spirit, and that other unseemly behaviour was being tolerated. The truth had to come out—and so with this unhappy background to the story Dennis Bennett stood in the pulpit on Passion Sunday and in a gentle unemotional fashion told his congregation about the experience which had transformed his life and that of many others in the church. The results already described followed.

Two days later Dennis wrote a letter to all his parishioners in an attempt to straighten out what had become a most confusing state of affairs:

My dear people:

I suppose that you know by now that I was asked to resign as rector of St. Mark's, and that I consented feeling that it would be more strategic for all concerned. My resignation has not been officially accepted as yet, so I still address you as rector of the parish. Since this is a personal statement, it is not coming to you at parish expense. I am well aware that many are painfully confused at the events of Sunday, and I would like to try to throw a little light on matters. This is a purely spiritual issue, and not one of personal animosity at all.

The New Testament, that part of the Holy Bible which tells us of the life of Jesus, and the doings of the early Christians, is a book crammed full of joy, power and love. We read of very ordinary, human people, making mistakes, getting into difficulties, having to be reprimanded, but all the while *knowing* that God had chosen them to be His children, and citizens of heaven, and "tasting the powers of the world to come". Miracles, healing, etc., were everyday events to them, for they walked in a world of wonder. If you will read your New Testaments and especially the first chapters of the Acts of the Apostles, and the letters of St. Paul, you will see that I am right. And it is not surprising that it should be so, for Jesus Himself promised it.

And when we come to ask how this can be, the answer

is: by the power of God the Holy Spirit, Who was able to pour Himself out in power upon the world after Jesus had died, risen again and ascended back to the Father. Jesus promised to his disciples: "Ye shall receive power, after that the Holy Ghost is come upon you, and ye shall be witnesses to Me...." Read St. John 14: 15–29. These are the words of Jesus, and they were spoken, not just to the first disciples, but to all believers in Jesus. And on the Day of Pentecost this promise of Christ was fulfilled, the Holy Spirit came with power, and the disciples were filled with His joy, and went out to bring the gospel (the good news) to everyone (Acts 2).

But what has happened to this joy and power and peace? What has happened to miracles, healing and all the other gifts of the Spirit that we are promised in the Holy Bible? Let us frankly admit that they are not seen much in the Church today. For most of us, religion is a plodding thing, resting on the grim determination of man, rather than the power of God, and yet Jesus said His yoke was easy and His burden light ... and "Fear not little flock, for it is your Father's good pleasure to *give* you the Kingdom." He did not say that we should be without troubles in the world, but He did say that our hearts would rejoice and that no man could take away our joy.

I have been pondering these things for a long time, but about five months ago, I received a spiritual experience that made me realise what was missing, and that is precisely the power of God the Holy Spirit in our lives. We talk about Him, but we don't know Him, and recognise His work in us as we should. He does not *fill* us, as the Bible says He will do, so instead of living by the power of God in us, we try to follow God's *rules* by our own power. In the words of the Bible we are still living by law, and not by faith.

I further became aware that the Episcopal Church clearly teaches that the Holy Spirit is to be received with power, for surely this is what the service of confirmation means. When, in the New Testament, the apostles laid their hands on newly baptised Christians, something very dramatic happened ... there was such an infilling with

65

power and joy and praise of God that again and again we read: "And they spake with tongues, and magnified God." On one occasion the result of the laying on of hands was so dramatic that a bystander pulled out his wallet and offered the apostles money "so that on whomsoever I lay hands they may receive the Holy Ghost".

I met some people, about five months ago, Episcopalians, who had received the fullness of the Holy Spirit. (I have since found that many Episcopalians, both clergy and people, know about this, but have been fearful of telling about it, for exactly the reason that you see now at St. Mark's—people just don't understand). I talked with these folks, and found that they did have this joy and power and peace that was so lacking in the lives of most Christians. They explained to me how they had received the Holy Spirit into their lives, and I followed their instruction, and received the power of the Holy Spirit into my life in a new and fuller way. The key to it, I found, is *praise*. It is in praising God that we enable Him to respond to us.

But it was here that the real centre of controversy came into the picture. I had never understood the meaning of the gift of unknown tongues, which is so much talked about in the New Testament, and which St. Paul says, by the command of the Lord, he would like to see every Christian receive (1 Cor. 14). I had, as I am sure many of you do, associated this gift with religious frenzy and fanaticism, and never thought it might have spiritual importance. But when I prayed for God to grant me the fullness of the Spirit, and opened my mouth to praise Him, I found to my amazement that as I repeated words of praise, the Holy Spirit did take my lips and tongue and form a new, and powerful language of praise and prayer that I myself could not understand, and that as I so praised God in whatever words or language he chose to use was a vitally important key to the receiving of the fullness of the Holy Spirit, for the Bible says that our tongue—our faculty of speech, is at the same time the best member of our body and also the most wicked, a "fire", a "world of iniquity". When you consider the harm that we can do with words, and the way in which we deceive and temporise with words, it is not unusual that we should be asked to let our faculty of speech be used by God to His glory—in the way that He chooses—before we can have His fullness.

Several people from the parish received this gift of the Holy Spirit at about the same time I did, and all of us were filled with joy at what we had found. We soon discovered, however, that others were not necessarily going to feel the same way, and that the question of the unknown tongue would be misunderstood. I attempted to keep the issue from coming to a head, and in so doing made matters far worse, because when something is secret there is an immediate implication that it is wrong. I finally saw that I had to tell you exactly what had happened to me, in order to clarify matters. There is, of course, much more to be said—books could be, and will be written on the subject. Just these few things right now.

I am sorry for the furor, and for the pain that has been caused. I ask every person in St. Mark's, whether they be for me or against me, *not to leave the parish or cancel their pledge*. This is a spiritual issue, and will not be settled in this way. I myself am going to stay strictly out of parish work until the matter has been clarified one way or the other. Support whatever interim pastorate the bishop and vestry set up. The matter will be straightened out before too long, and life will go on at St. Mark's.

Any rumours that reach your ears that in any way imply that I am leaving the Episcopal Church are false. For example, there is a rumour being circulated that I was recently rebaptised in another denomination! This, I am sure you will know, is *nonsense*. What I am standing for is to be found within the Episcopal Church; no one needs to leave the Episcopal Church in order to have the fullness of the Spirit. But it is important that the Spirit be allowed to work freely in the Episcopal Church, and it is to this that I bear witness, and will continue to bear witness.

St. Mark's is not alone in this. I am not alone in this. I know of dozens of Episcopal parishes throughout the country where the work of the Holy Spirit is known in just this same way. I know of dozens of Episcopal clergy who know about it all, and rejoice in their knowledge. Just this morning I received word from the pastor of a very large Lutheran church in this area asking, "What are the Episcopalians so excited about? We have had people in our parish for a long time who have the gift of tongues. It's wonderful. Why are you fighting about it?"

I remind you that we are not alone in this. The work of the Holy Spirit in this way is quite widely known in the Episcopal Church, and also in other established denominations, but up to now it has been kept a secret, and Pentecost was no secret. "These things were not done in a corner," as St. Paul says. It seems that God has chosen St. Mark's as one of the places for this all-important issue to become a matter of common knowledge and discussion. Read your Bibles, and especially read: Mark 16: 17–18, Luke 11: 9–13, John 7: 37–39, John 1: 32–34, John 14: 10–29, John 15: 20–27, John 16: 7–15, Acts 1: 5–8, Acts 2: 1–18, Acts 2: 38–39, Acts 8, Acts 10, Acts 19: 1–6, 1 Corinthians, chapters 12, 13 and 14. Read chapter 14 very carefully, and note that St. Paul says that it is the "command of the Lord", and that Paul does not in any sense minimise or condemn the use of the unknown tongue. He asks only for orderliness.

Think about it. Pray about it. This is a vital spiritual issue. Many of you have known me for years, and I think you know that I would not have so disturbed this parish for any but the most urgent reasons. I am ready to talk with anyone who wishes to talk with me, but I am not going to enter into any public controversy about the matter. Whether you think I am right or wrong, please pray and work for the peace of God's people, and for the enlightenment of God's people. May God bless you all, however you may feel about all this.

"Hear the words of the evangelist St. Luke, in the eighth chapter of the Acts of the Apostles.

"When the apostles which were at Jerusalem heard that Samaria had received the word of God, they sent unto them Peter and John: who, when they were come down, prayed for them that they might receive the Holy Ghost: for as yet He was fallen upon none of them, only they were

68

baptised in the name of the Lord Jesus. Then laid they their hands on them, and they received the Holy Ghost." (From the Order of Confirmation, p. 296, The Book of Common Prayer according to the use of the Protestant Episcopal Church in the United States of America.)

. . .

It would clearly have been better to have brought the issue into the open as soon as it had begun to affect members of the church. But it is easy to be wise after the event, and the situation was very novel. Those involved tried sincerely and charitably to avoid making the matter an issue in the church. But unwittingly their action made it harder to face when eventually the facts became known to all.

But in a strange and wonderful way this sad story has a happy ending. Dennis Bennett found himself without a job and branded throughout the Episcopal Church as a religious crank. No one was in much of a hurry to invite him to be their rector.

Then the late Bishop of Olympia, Bishop Lewis, took the initiative and invited Dennis to be vicar of St. Luke's Episcopal church, Seattle. "When you come, Dennis," he said, "bring the fire with you—you'll need it up there." It was just what Dennis had been praying for. St. Luke's was a very different proposition from St. Mark's. It had after fifty years' or so existence still not attained parish status. It was still a mission church, without making any noticeable impact on the community in fifty years. Requests had been received by the bishop to close it down, it was such a hopeless flop. There was no hope that it would ever get off the ground.

When Dennis arrived on July 1st, 1960, few would have exactly envied him his task. The church was disillusioned and confused. The budget was $18,000, but by December only $12,000 had come in. It was bankrupt in more ways than one.

Twelve months later the Holy Spirit had done a miracle. By then eighty-five out of the two hundred communicants had been filled with the Holy Spirit—practically the whole inner core of the church. Church attendance had multiplied many times over. They had wanted to pull the church down because it was redundant—now they wanted to pull it down because it was not big enough to get all the people in. The budget had been increased by fifty per cent and all the bills were paid. Since then a new church hall has been built, entirely paid for by the gifts of the congregation. A new sense of love and unity pervaded the church. There had been no division. Two hundred people now attended the mid-week fellowship meeting, and lay people were taking responsibility for much of the work of the church.

Mrs. Jean Stone wrote about this exciting story in *Trinity* magazine: "A small episcopal mission without love, without power, without the peace of God, is being converted by the power of God into a thriving church with the gifts and fruit of the Spirit being manifested in the lives of the parishioners."

It is such stories, rather than individual testimonies, which are the best advertisement for the miracles which the Holy Spirit can perform.

CHAPTER NINE

THIS IS THAT

THE story of Dennis Bennett and how he came into this movement is only a fraction of the whole story. Without soliciting it, he got the publicity and the knocks—and they usually go together. We are too close to these events to get them into true perspective. As any photographer knows, focusing is always more difficult on near than on distant objects. To make it even more difficult, the subject is constantly moving. We are looking at a widespread kaleidoscope of Christians looking for the answers in a world increasingly biased against the Christian message. It is like one of those Dutch paintings—full of multitudinous activity—rather than a Rembrandt portrait.

It is all about fallible human beings, so it includes many mistakes and corrections. But whether we take one glance or study the subject thoroughly, the general impression is of wholesome goodness.

Your sons ... shall prophesy

There is a fascinating link with the past in the so-called Shakarian story. A number of years before the Azusa Street meetings there had been outbreaks of revival in various parts of the Balkans and Russia. Those involved had spoken in tongues and prophesied, as well as experiencing the other gifts of the Holy Spirit. In 1855 an eleven-year-old illiterate Russian boy who lived in Armenia had a most unusual experience. For a whole week he appeared to be under the power of God and wrote down prophecies of future events. He drew pictures, maps and charts foretelling a great war and the invasion of Armenia by the Turks. The Christians were warned that they would be murdered if they did not leave Armenia and cross the seas to another land. The maps revealed that this land would be America. Apparently this evidence was carefully preserved by the

Armenians and never forgotten. They waited for the next step to be revealed to them.

In the Armenian town of Kara Kala there lived a Presbyterian family called Shakarian. They were among the first to receive the Pentecostal experience. There was great sadness in the family because they had no son. In May 1891 a great-uncle visited the family, and one day as he was sitting reading the Bible he received sudden inspiration. He immediately got to his feet and went over to Mrs. Shakarian and said to her: "God has heard your prayer. One year from this day you will be the mother of a son."

Exactly one year later, on May 25th, 1892, a son was born, and what better could they have done than call him Isaac, for like Abraham's son he was a son of promise.

In 1900 the same young illiterate peasant, now a man in his fifties, began to speak again to his friends and neighbours. He warned them that the time was fast approaching when these strange prophecies would be fulfilled, and urged them to leave Armenia immediately. So that year the exodus to America began, and they took the written prophecies with them.

Five years later the Shakarians packed up their things, sold their land and left Kara Kala to settle eventually in Los Angeles. Their sudden evacuation must have amused their sceptical countrymen, but by 1912 the last Pentecostal family had left—in the nick of time as events were to prove. When the First World War broke out in 1914 the Turks crushed Armenia and over three million Armenians were murdered, including those who stayed in Kara Kala.

But the home of the Shakarians became a church for the immigrant Armenians and Russians in Los Angeles. One day Mr Demos Shakarian, Isaac's father, went for a walk in the city with two friends. As they chatted together they happened to pass Azusa Street and heard a noise which was strangely familiar coming from an old tumbledown wooden building. Taking a look inside they were surprised to discover a service in progress very similar to the one they had become used to in Armenia. So two streams converged at Azusa Street—but that is not the end of the story.

In 1912 the just-come-of-age son of the Shakarians

married and took his young bride Edna to Downey in California. Isaac had saved just enough money to buy a piece of land and three Holstein cows. There he opened the Reliance Dairy. By 1943 it had become the world's largest independent dairy, with three thousand cows.

The story now switches to Isaac's son Demos, who had been named after his grandfather. Unlike his father he seemed to make a real hash of business. A few years after getting married he was in financial straits. He turned to his father to help him over the dollar problem—but to God to rescue him from his sense of failure and frustration. He began open-air preaching. This was a turning point in his life: "It took all the starch and pride out of me and I learned about the needs of the people there. From that time on I have never been afraid of man. Whether he is a ruler or a labourer, I know he needs God; it is easy for me to talk to him about the Lord."

From open-air meetings he turned to sponsoring revival meetings, and became interested in the work of the Christian Business Men's Committee. Gradually the idea of a Pentecostal businessmen's group crystallised in his mind. In 1951 he shared his vision with Oral Roberts, who encouraged him to go ahead. A little later that year he planned the first meeting, to which twenty-one people came.

But for the next year or so nothing seemed to go right. There were more discouragements and frustrations than blessings. Demos began to doubt. Had his vision really been from God? Was he making a big mistake? As once before in his life he became haunted with the spectre of failure. Even his wife thought he was on the wrong track.

Then one Friday night he brought the matter to God in prayer. He told his wife that he was going to the front room: "I'm not leaving," he added, "until I hear from heaven."

Then he prayed and wept before God until 3 o'clock the next morning. By this time his wife was getting a bit anxious, so she tiptoed into the room and started to play the organ. Suddenly she stopped playing and began to speak in tongues and prophesy: "Because you have been

73

faithful in little things I am going to use you in a greater way . . ." went the prophecy.

Then Demos saw a vision: "It was as though there was no ceiling in the room and I was looking out on the world. I saw millions of men—no women—just men. Their arms were folded and their heads were bowed low as though they were dead. My wife, who had no idea what I was seeing, continued her interpretation: 'and then the very thing you see before you now, will soon come to pass.' Suddenly the whole vision was electrified. The millions of dead men threw up their hands and started magnifying God."

This was the second great turning point in Demos's life. The same morning at the businessmen's meeting everything seemed to go right. In 1953 the Full Gospel Business Men's Fellowship International (F.G.B.M.F.I.) really got off the ground under the presidency of Demos Shakarian, and it has never looked back.

It is not only its voluminous name which makes people think twice. Its remarkable success does too. Its magazine *Voice* has a monthly circulation of over a quarter of a million copies. It has now branched out too with a magazine for young people and one for those with high intelligence quotas. It has branches or chapters all over America and Canada—and other parts of the world, including Holland, Switzerland, Hong Kong and South Africa. It has played a not insignificant part in the movement in the historic churches as well as in the Pentecostal denominations. Many ministers and lay people from the churches have attended the breakfasts and luncheons of the Fellowship and received the experience of the Baptism in the Spirit.

What is the secret of the success of this organisation? Perhaps, to put it very simply, it has met a need and met it well. It is a lay movement free from the shackles of ecclesiastical sanctions. One of the principal features of the contemporary Church is the growing emancipation of the layman—the taking out of the deep freeze of what Hendrick Kraemer has called "the Church's frozen assets". the businessmen run the organisation and they invite the ministers to do the speaking. This is apostolic commonsense. The apostles in their day refused even to do social work—their function was "prayer and the ministry of the word". There are many laymen the world over who are sick and tired of anaemic watered-down Christianity—and are usually very nice about it. There are churches—as Billy Graham has put it—"more interested in statistics and meeting the budget than they are in spiritual power". Ministers are often in an invidious position, bound by ties of loyalty which hinder them from taking a lead when they might like to do so. They are often part of an out-of-date ecclesiastical system. But the layman is much freer, and the F.G.B.M.F.I. is one expression of a desire to use this freedom in a responsible and meaningful manner.

It is significant too that Demos saw only men in his vision! Modern Christianity looks to many outsiders like a closed shop for women. Most churches are dominated numerically by women. F.G.B.M.F.I. should serve a useful function in redressing the balance a bit and injecting a little more masculinity into church life.

So three generations of Shakarians have shared in a Pentecostal pilgrimage which has taken them from Kara Kala in the heart of Russia to the old stable in Azusa Street, and from there into most of the major banqueting halls in the United States. It is quite a story.

. . . and your daughters shall prophesy

One of the most active members of St. Mark's church, Van Nuys, was the wife of a Lockheed Corporation executive. Her name is Jean Stone. For several years she had been aware that something was missing in her life. She did not then know what it was. She attended all the services she could, read the Bible regularly, prayed at various times every day and served in many of the organisations of her church.

"There was still a void in my life which nothing but more of Him could fill," she wrote. So she figured out that she must have missed God's best for her life. Being a woman she was barred from the priesthood, married from being a nun—and her husband was not likely at this stage in his life to become a missionary. There was nothing she could do now to put this right.

The turning point came when together with others from St. Mark's she attended a retreat. The speaker said something which struck a chord in some of those present: "The Church," he said, "ought to ask to be forgiven for its sin of neglecting the Holy Spirit." For Jean Stone, as for the others, the Holy Spirit was practically unknown. So they began to pray that the Holy Spirit would come to their church, not knowing what this was going to mean to some of them. The prayer was answered, though not in the way they expected.

In the spring of 1961 the first edition of the *Trinity* magazine was published by the Blessed Trinity Society, which was founded by Mrs. Jean Stone. As a religious quarterly it has circled the globe and has made a real impact with its forthright no-nonsense articles and helpful testimonies. It is dedicated to "maintaining the fullness of the faith". Its message is particularly geared to the historic denominations and pleads for a restoration of the Holy Spirit to His rightful regnancy in the life and experience of the Church and its members. It has played a significant part in bringing the news of this revival to church members all over the world. It had a vital ministry in Britain, as we shall see later.

There is an infectious simplicity about Jean Stone's approach which is deceptive, for there is nothing naïve or shallow in it. When you talk to her you find she seems to know most of the answers and to have a very firm grasp of the theology behind the experience and gifts of the Holy Spirit. She had no previous editorial or business experience when she took on the job of producing the *Trinity* magazine. It seems to find its way sooner or later on to the desks of most ministers in the Western hemisphere and seldom ends up in the wastepaper basket. It gets more and more dog-eared as it passes from vicarage to manse, and usually dies of sheer exhaustion at a ripe old age. Anglican bishops (publish it not in Gath) have surreptitiously read it and passed it on to their chaplains.

One day at the height of the battle provoked by Bishop James Pike's pastoral letter, banning the promotion of "speaking in tongues" in his diocese, Jean Stone's photograph appeared next to the bishop's in a front-page article in the San Francisco *Sunday Chronicle*. The bishop is glaring—Jean smiling. Underneath the bishop's picture were the words "fighting the trend", and under Jean's "spreading the Word". In the controversy which has followed this clash Jean Stone and others have been commendably calm and charitable without withdrawing from their insistence on the importance of what is happening for the whole Church of God.

... Your young men shall see visions ...

In September 1962 Mrs. Jean Stone received a letter from Bob Morris, a student at Yale University and a member of the Yale Inter-Varsity Christian Fellowship. He told her that some of the students had come to realise that there was something important missing in their lives which hindered their witnessing and living the Christian life they knew they should before their fellow students.

"Frankly, Mrs. Stone," the letter went on, "we want the infilling so that we can join in this wonderful revival God is sending on His Church. We do not know what sort of trouble the Holy Spirit's denouement on the campus would bring, but I think we are willing to risk it ... please send someone to us as soon as possible...."

Jean Stone took immediate action and within a week Harald Bredesen, minister of the First Reformed Church of Mount Vernon, New York, had extricated himself from a busy life and arrived on the campus. That evening they met eight of the students in a top floor room, and six received the Baptism in the Spirit. Seven more received a little later and the news began to get around. The chaplains were a bit nonplussed, but there was no opposition. One young man's parents were so concerned about what had just happened to their son that they wrote to the world-famous church historian, Dr. K. S. Latourette. Back came the answer, "This is quite evidently a work of the Spirit." Bishop Lesslie Newbigin came to investigate and prayed with the students.

The story of how top-class intellectuals were experiencing these things soon spread to other universities, with requests for meetings, and the same results followed. Students began to testify: "The Bible is now a living thing ..."; "the whole thing is like driving a nitroglycerine truck down a dirt road. At any moment ..."; "It did not prove to be the emotional cataclysm I had been expecting ... but a new ability to give praise which seems to flow out of unknown depths in a non-emotional but full self-filling way ..."; "As the gift was increasingly exercised, the sense of communion with the Lord and a deepening of joy and stability increased. I found that my mental awareness was in no way erased by this ..."; "It has brought increasing unity and love to us here ..."; "The revolutionary power to witness to the revolutionary Christ and the insight and guidance to walk in the path of discipleship have been part of the work of the Spirit in me ..."; "In this way I have come to know God in His fullness, all of His trinitarian majesty. He has brought me awe of the Father, love of the Son, and joy of the Spirit."

These are some fragments from the account the students themselves gave of what had happened to them. Three weeks after sending the first letter Bob Morris wrote to Jean Stone: "Thank God for your quick response to my letter ... honestly I just can't get over it."

"There ought to be something that distinguishes the Church of Jesus Christ from a Rotary Club," cracked a minister according to a full-length report of the movement in the American magazine *Saturday Evening Post* by McCandlish Phillips.[7] When Peter had the job of explaining "speaking in tongues" to the flabbergasted crowd on the Day of Pentecost he began by saying, "This is that ..." and went on to explain it in terms of an ancient prophecy that God's people would receive power of an unusual nature before the end of the age, "the great and manifest day". Are we seeing a more comprehensive fulfilment of what was only partial on the Day of Pentecost? Whether this is true or not, few Christians would seriously question the desperate need of the Church for fresh power and inspiration.

The former Dean of Detroit Cathedral, the Very Rev.

John J. Weaver, comments on this in the same magazine: "The disease today is nihilism—nothingness. And I don't mean philosophical nihilism; I mean lived nihilism, the kind you find in hospital beds, in the office. The problem today is lack of power, Spirit. The bones are dry and dead. We need a new strengthening of the Spirit. I think the reason we are seeing speaking in tongues today is that the world is so fragmented and torn, and in the midst of all this loneliness and fragmentation the Christian needs a fresh indwelling of the Holy Spirit. I don't think the Christians were singing Quo Vadis in the Colosseum; I think they were praising the Lord in tongues...."[7]

Morton Kelsey tells us in his book [8] of how an Episcopal minister was summarily dismissed from his post because someone he ministered to received the gift of tongues. Other clergy sprang to his defence and quoted St. Paul's direction not to forbid speaking in tongues. A church spokesman caustically replied: "Yes, but times have changed. St. Paul isn't the bishop here." It may all seem incongruous in the pattern of what Bishop Sterling of Montana in his forthright manner calls "Episcopal respectabilianism". Times certainly have changed, but we could well do with a few St. Pauls today to wake us up. The "this" of our modern church life is nothing like the "that" of apostolic Christianity. Maybe this movement has been sent by God to restore the incongruity.

CHAPTER TEN

ATLANTIC CROSSING

A YOUNG man knocked apprehensively at the door of an English Midland rectory. Ron had received a mysterious message from the rector asking him to come to see him. He had been a Christian for only a few years, but at school he had met a young fellow who had obviously a richer experience of God than he had. He was inquisitive. His interest grew when he heard from this friend about the Baptism in the Spirit which had been one of the secrets of the power of the early Church. He wanted this experience for himself. One day during the school lunch break Ron and his friend went out into the fields for prayer, and there he received the power which Christ promised to those who believed on Him. His girl friend Margaret received this gift a short time afterwards.

They were staunch members of their local Anglican church, and felt it right to tell their rector and his wife immediately. The news was received with interest but no apparent enthusiasm. So the thought which was dominant in Ron's mind as he made his way to the rectory was that he was about to receive his "marching orders". After all, "speaking in tongues" was hardly respectable for members of an Anglican church, and the rector knew that he and his friend were active and influential leaders among the young people who came to the church. He imagined that the rector would politely tell them to leave.

The door opened and the rector ushered a rather tense young man into the lounge, where his wife Nora was sitting. Ron braced himself for the inevitable ultimatum.

"Will you pray for us," the rector said, "for we want this blessing too."

In great excitement Ron fetched his friend Margaret, and there in the lounge of the rectory the four knelt in prayer. It was September 28th, 1962—almost three years after Dennis Bennett had humbly knelt before his lay friends John and Joan Baker.

The rector wrote later: "I had always been on my guard against any form of emotionalism ... but I felt sure I would be safe in my own lounge. Ron prayed for me and laid his hands upon me, while Margaret prayed for my wife. Ron prayed and praised in English and then softly in other tongues, which I now heard for the first time, but I wasn't put off! Then God worked the miracle. His Holy Spirit in all His mighty power just filled the room and came upon me. I was filled with deep joy and overflowing praise."

His wife entered into the same blessing, both of them speaking in tongues as the Spirit gave them utterance.

God had been preparing the rector for some time and the testimony of these two young people had struck a chord in his life. Overburdened and strained with parish duties, which seemed profitless and unrewarding, he was conscious of spiritual lethargy and a lack of real Christian joy and peace. When news percolated through of happenings in the Episcopal Church of America he showed increasing interest. The final straw came when in September 1962 Dr. Philip Hughes wrote an editorial in the *Churchman*, an Evangelical quarterly, painting a glowing picture of the work of the Holy Spirit, following a personal visit to California at the invitation of Mrs. Jean Stone. He knew there must be something in it.

So things were beginning to happen in England too.

Wimpole Street in the West End of London is a far cry from the slag heaps of that Midland town. Arriving at his office on Monday morning August 27th, 1962, an architect found lying there a copy of *Trinity* magazine given him by a friend. He read it with great interest.

He had been a lifelong member of the Church of England and a Christian for as long as he could remember. His father had been a clergyman. But in 1960 an interest in divine healing drove him to search for the secret of spiritual power. He became jaded as his search seemed to be getting him nowhere. Five times he had hands laid on him for the Baptism in the Spirit.

He slipped the *Trinity* magazine into his brief-case before leaving the office to catch the train home. He read it all the way home, and after dinner in his study until he went to bed about a quarter to eleven. His son was away for the night and his wife had gone to bed early and was by this time fast asleep. He ran his bath water and was soon relaxing in the bath. Then the miracle happened. He sighed to God his deep longing. He had recently heard of someone who had received this experience in the bathroom. "If only I could speak like——." Suddenly a flow of language which he had never heard before began to issue from his mouth. It came effortlessly.

"I was speaking as easily as though I were speaking English. Though the language was unintelligible to me, it was definitely a language. The rather strange thing about this which I had not expected was that this was quite unemotional, except for controlled joy and the edification spoken of by Paul. My mind was perfectly clear and I was listening with great interest and noticing recurring phrases. Although I could not at that moment speak a word of English, I nevertheless was giving praise to Jesus with my conscious mind. I was also thinking quite practically while the flow continued inexorably."

So he continued for an hour in praise and prayer, and then for his wife's sake went to bed, although he felt he could have continued all night.

Here was another link in a chain which was beginning to form across Britain as in the United States and elsewhere.

The *Trinity* magazine played a part in the next story too. This time it concerns a young Presbyterian minister in Scotland. The same preparation was being experienced before the blessing came.

"I was often almost cross-eyed looking at the perfect ideal and fact of Jesus on the one hand and my own shortcomings on the other," he wrote of his preparation for this experience. He wanted to be more "devout". But then he looked at the devoted religious people who seemed so joyless, and shuddered. That was not the way for him. He examined his ministry critically. Preaching? Well, he at least did not bore people. Praying? Not regularly, but he was trying hard. Visiting the sick? He hated it. He always felt so helpless and the whole business seemed pointless. Visiting the congregation was dull. He did not really care for them. Altogether a pretty devastating cross-examination—but he was at least being honest with himself.

In 1961 he sent his Whitsun sermon to a friend for comment. Back it came: "A mockery of the life-giving Holy Spirit! Deadly dull." He realised he wasn't even a good preacher. The numbers in his church began to drop. He expected this during the summer months. But in the autumn they still continued to drop. That autumn he heard a layman say that the Church of Scotland was dying. The ministers had the right message, but they were sleepless at night because it wasn't going over to the congregation. That hit him hard too, for he had to admit that he wasn't sleepless at night. Then his terrible complacency dawned on him—he just didn't care enough.

He began to do what one would normally assume that every minister did—pray every morning. He did not understand then what he really wanted. He simply asked God, "Make me a clean heart and renew a right spirit within me. Oh, give me the comfort of thy help again, and stablish me with thy free spirit."

About this time a friend of his studying theology at Edinburgh University wrote and told him about a group which was praying for a deeper knowledge of the Holy Spirit. It suddenly came to him that as far as he was concerned the Holy Spirit was just the third person of a theological concept. So he decided that the best thing to do was to begin to preach about the Holy Spirit, until he realised that he was only doing what he had so often been guilty of before—blaming his congregation for his own personal inadequacies. He therefore began to pray and preach for power.

Then his friend called to see him and the first rays of light pierced the darkness of his position. The friend directed him to the Acts of the Apostles and the experience which the Church had forgotten about, but which had been important to the apostles and one of the secrets of their

83

power. Then he told him what had been happening in the Episcopal Church of America. It was all news to him. When his friend left he went straight to his Bible and searched carefully, then he began to pray eagerly, expectantly and sincerely for the Holy Spirit to come and revitalise his powerless ministry.

Almost immediately things began to happen. For the first time in his life the Bible became the Word of God to him. He began to experience guidance and there was a new hope and purpose in life. His faith began to grow. Then the American magazine *Trinity* came into his hands and he read it from cover to cover. God began to reveal to him the truths about divine healing.

On Sunday, May 27th, 1962, after the evening service, he retired alone to his study. He picked up *Trinity* and began to read it, and as he read he felt a sudden impulse to fall on his knees. As he did so, he received his Baptism in the Holy Spirit. The presence of Christ was so real and his joy so deep that he was almost weeping with exhilaration. Then he began to speak in other tongues.

The climate of opinion in Britain was against such a movement until the sixties. The Pentecostals, as we have seen, are weaker here than in the United States, and initially suffered more persecution and ostracism. News from the United States was taken by most with a pinch of salt, and very little happened until 1962. In that year the three stories we have related took place in different parts of the country without any link between them, though all three were in some way influenced by the American events. They were the firstfruits of an increasingly extensive harvest in the churches of Britain.

It is very difficult to assess all this, as one is seeing the beginnings of a new movement and the scene is constantly changing. But from 1962 onwards there has been a steady increase in interest and support. Minds previously shut completely to this subject have become open, even though many are cautious and unwilling to commit themselves in support or opposition.

Apart from a short visit in 1960 by David du Plessis, no

one from the United States had visited Britain to speak about what was happening on the other side of the Atlantic. But in May 1963 the Rev. Frank Maguire visited Britain on holiday and spoke at various meetings. He addressed a privately convened ministers' meeting in London, where interest was shown. Later he spoke at the Church Army Training College, where a student received the experience in his bedroom a short time after the meeting. A very small meeting was arranged in an Oxfordshire village and after it Mr. Maguire prayed with a few people who received the blessing and spoke in tongues. He preached too in a West-End Anglican Church, but his visit did not cause much more than a rippling of ecclesiastical waters. Some interest was aroused, but others were sceptical. Most people did not want to commit themselves to something which was so new, but rather desired time to think out the theological and pastoral implications.

There was one factor which helped to change the reserve of many. This was the visit of Dr. Philip Hughes to America earlier in 1962. He was in Washington D.C. when he received an invitation from Mrs. Jean Stone to visit California and see things for himself. Mrs. Stone had read an article in *Christianity Today* by Dr. Hughes and had no idea that an Anglican could be so Evangelical. Dr. Hughes had a few days to spare, so accepted willingly the opportunity of investigating at first hand what he had heard so much about.

He was profoundly impressed by what he saw. He attended some of the prayer groups and spoke at length with Mrs. Stone. He witnessed the manifestation of the gifts of the Spirit in these Episcopalian gatherings, and was gratified to notice that everything was done decently and in order and in full conformity with the instructions given by Paul in 1 Corinthians 12 and 14. In his own words, he had attributed what he heard "to a flirtation under the hot Californian sun with the extravagances of Pentecostalism", but now that he had seen it for himself the half had not been told him.

Dr. Hughes is an Evangelical scholar, with a distinct leaning towards Reformed convictions. As early as 1947 he wrote a small booklet on the subject of revival and has a deep longing for it. He is Editor of the *Churchman*, a quarterly theological journal, and so when he returned to his flat in Kensington Square he wrote an enthusiastic editorial about his visit.

"There are already indications of a new movement of the Holy Spirit within the Church at the present time. Is this something for which we are ready? Are we willing, do we long, for a divine tide of blessing to flow over us? *That tide is even now on its way.*" This was published in September 1962.

Here was Dr. Hughes's estimate of the situation in the United States, and coming from the pen of such a sane and balanced theologian it caused many to sit up and take notice. He disarmed the prejudices of many by this forthright editorial. It was to be reprinted and distributed very widely—over 60,000 copies being sold in the autumn of 1962 and in 1963.

In the summer of 1963 a young Lutheran theologian and pastor called Larry Christenson, and his wife, left San Pedro in California for the Lutheran World Conference being held in Helsinki. On their way home Larry spoke at meetings in Germany and then spent a few days in London. Again a private meeting was convened for ministers in the afternoon and lay people in the evening. A further step forward was taken and the interest was growing. Before he left there were two curates on the staff of an Anglican Church in London who had entered into this blessing. A young Anglo-Catholic vicar was present at the ministers' meeting and after Larry Christenson had finished speaking he humbly confessed his personal need for this blessing. Within a few weeks he received the Baptism in the Spirit with the gift of tongues, and before many months were past a number more of the clergy of his diocese had entered into the experience.

Some time before this visit Larry Christenson had written a small booklet on the gift of tongues called *Speaking in tongues, a gift for the Body of Christ*. It was destined to have a remarkable ministry throughout the world. The Christian girl who typed the manuscript for the

German translation was speaking in tongues herself before she had finished. In the autumn of 1963 it was published in Britain and soon had a wide circulation.

Christenson's visit to London was at the end of August. A month or so later David du Plessis spent a few days in London en route for the United States after a visit to Holland. When it was known that he would be in London a meeting was arranged in a West-End hotel and several hundred invitations sent out before he could be contacted. Du Plessis spoke to a packed audience for nearly two hours. He received an enthusiastic response and after the meeting a few more were to receive the experience of the Spirit's fullness.

So, slowly but surely, the movement of the Holy Spirit continued. There was mounting interest and very little opposition. Early in 1964 the well-known magazine *Crusade* carried two articles by the Rev. Hywel Davies, an Elim minister and Administrative Secretary of the Evangelical Alliance. Interest began to develop in the Baptist denomination and several ministers entered into blessing. *Trinity* magazine was sold in this country and many copies were in constant circulation. There were no official pronouncements from church leaders.

In the spring of 1964 Don Stone had to make a business trip to Europe, which included London. He was increasingly concerned about the health of his wife Jean and thought the change would do her good. She arrived in London to discover that an extensive itinerary had been worked out for her, including a press conference, two public meetings in London, a trip to Scotland and visits to Bradford, Stoke-on-Trent and several other places. It was a great success—the itinerary that is, not Jean Stone's nice prospect of a rest. In Scotland nearly fifty people were prayed for and received the blessing, including several ministers.

In London it was the first public meeting arranged by non-Pentecostals since the days of Alexander Boddy and Cecil Polhill. It was held in the Caxton Hall—so frequently used fifty years ago by Boddy and Polhill. A large number came to hear Jean Stone and over fifty received the

Spirit's fullness. Mrs. Stone began her talk in a most un-usual way. During the preliminaries she received an "anointing" to speak in tongues. She waited patiently until it was her turn to speak, then she explained graciously what she was going to do. With every head bowed and a hush of expectancy she spoke in tongues. Then someone from the audience gave the interpretation. It was followed by two further manifestations of tongues and interpretation from the audience, the three together seeming to be a divinely-appointed seal at this stage.

In the summer of 1964 David du Plessis spent a month in this country and spoke at many meetings. He attended the General Assembly of the Church of Scotland in Edin-burgh. A remarkable meeting was held in Luton, to which all the clergy of the St. Albans Diocese were invited, the Bishop of Bedford was in the chair, and a large number of clergy attended. Great interest was shown.

At the time of writing over a hundred ministers of all denominations in Britain have had this experience, and of that number only two are known to have lost their appoint-ments as a result of this issue. The movement is staying firmly in the churches and many hundreds of lay people are being led into blessing too. There has been friction and some division in a few churches, mainly caused by mis-placed zeal on the one hand and ignorance and fear on the other. On the whole there has been a remarkable growth in spiritual maturity among those groups which have de-veloped in the churches. In the Anglican Church there has been as much interest among Anglo-Catholics as among Evangelicals.

One significant feature is that young people are being much affected, and there is widespread interest in the theological and missionary training colleges. A number of missionaries have returned to their work abroad having experienced the Baptism in the Spirit in this country. In the closely knit community life of such colleges there have been difficulties, and again there has been the accusation of divisiveness.

It is impossible to give more than this brief account of happenings in Britain. The movement is far too young as yet to comment very decisively. But a great deal of what is going on has the hallmark of an authentic work of the Holy Spirit. One cannot help but be impressed with the spontaneity of interest and the sensible and balanced way in which Christians are behaving. There is little sign of that overweening pride and fanatical spirit which has wrecked so many good movements in the past. At least many people are thinking, watching, although not commenting too loudly.

PART THREE

APPRAISAL

CHAPTER ELEVEN

FACING FACTS

IT would be easy to dismiss all this as comparatively trivial and irrelevant—a kind of cul-de-sac leading nowhere and diverting Christians from the main line of realism. But such an attitude is impossible if we are prepared to face the facts.

To get to these we will have to strip off a good deal of camouflage which has covered the whole subject for years. The hoary old story of the Chinaman, who spoke in tongues and was found to be blaspheming God, dies hard. There are so many variations of this tale it makes one suspicious. It is amazing how this one story has been so successful in frightening honest people off the whole subject—even though the facts have probably never been substantiated.

When we look at literature we find the same prejudices. For example, there were manifestations of the Spirit, including speaking in tongues, during the Welsh revival of 1904–5, but there is no mention of this fact in the principal book which has been written about it—*The Awakening in Wales*, by Mrs. Penn-Lewis. The same gifts were also experienced during the revival which took place at Mukti in India, through the ministry of the well-known Pandita Ramabai. But in her biography, written by Helen S. Dyer, there is no mention of this.

This makes it all the harder to discover the facts and assess them properly. The Pentecostal Movement has developed quite separately from the rest of the Church and there is a great deal of ignorance about it. It has suffered more than its share of misrepresentation. But it has outlived its earliest opponents and is stronger today in many parts of the world than it has ever been. It has spread all over the world and, as we have seen, its influence is being felt in all the denominations. Canon Douglas Webster speaks of it in South America as "by far the most significant religious movement in the whole continent".[9]

The Pentecostal churches are the most missionary minded in the world. Their missionary methods have been first class. They have always sought to found truly indigenous churches, and leadership today is nearly always in the hands of the nationals. David du Plessis once commented on this while lecturing at Princeton Seminary in 1959: "The first forty years of my life I spent in Africa. I saw most of the missionaries trying to make 'foreigners' instead of Christians out of Africans. They took great pains to make them Roman Catholics, Lutherans, Calvinists and Methodists. Actually the worst was when there were some German Lutherans and other national brands of the same confession. My whole being rebelled against this kind of mission. Our Pentecostal Missions flourished because we did not have books or creeds or catechisms to teach the Africans. We gave them the Bible and told them to believe what is there, and the missionary lived the life that only the Holy Spirit can cause men to live. The Pentecostal Church among the Africans, and for that matter among most nations, becomes an indigenous Church with very little effort. The Holy Spirit creates these churches."

Today there are more Pentecostal missionaries on the field proportionately than any other church, and their church giving is considerably higher too. No wonder they are in some countries the fastest growing church.

The Movement has developed on a very simple theological basis, and it has so far produced no outstanding theologians. But in recent years it has tended to stress the need for theological training. Canon Douglas Webster draws attention to this "total lack of theology" as "quite the most serious"[9] weakness and defect of the movement. One wonders if he is right. Theology itself does not provide strength. There is good and bad theology. Bad theology can be more harmful than no theology at all. It is unfair to castigate Pentecostals for their lack of theology when one's own has often been damaging to faith and experience. The neglect, for example, of the doctrine of the Holy Spirit is one pertinent aspect of this. The churches have suffered enormously from modernism, which has tended to undermine the faith and power of the Church. The Pentecostals have not failed here yet. And in any case, as we shall see later, the theology of the Pentecostals may well be nearer to the truth than ours has been.

But it is no longer a matter of assessing a movement which is at a safe distance from one's own church. It is now entrenched in the main Protestant denominations. Morton Kelsey writes: "As long as the practice remained within the Holiness and Pentecostal churches, it could be ignored. But now both clergy whose excellence of training cannot be overlooked, and sophisticated laity in the major denominations, have spoken not only for the personal value of the experience, but of its theological significance."[10] This is important for the Christian Church, and it would be an act of irresponsibility for us to pass by on the other side of the road and ignore it. "It is no longer a phenomenon of some odd sect across the street," went an article in the Episcopalian magazine, *Living Church*, of July 17th, 1960—"it is in our midst and it is being practised by clergy and laity who have stature and good reputation in the Church."[11]

This movement has come at a time of real need in Britain. The Christian cause is not exactly thriving. There is a mood of depression in the Church today. Much has been tried—and it has largely failed to draw the people back to the churches. Humanism and agnosticism are no longer refuges for the mentally lazy—they are becoming militant forces in Britain. It has become fashionable to be an unbeliever.

"We all know that England is substantially a secular country," writes David L. Edwards in his book *The Honest to God Debate*. "Their unpopularity might not matter, and might actually redound to their credit—if the churches possessed an inner confidence. It might then be suggested that people are offended by the churches' stern integrity, as people were offended by Jesus Christ Himself. But as it is, we all know that, for all the devoted labour to be observed in them, the English churches need a revival. They are not aflame with faith or overflowing with purposeful activity. They offend England not because they are too lively but because most of them seem to have been decaying over the last half-century. This is why the stage is set in our time for a new Christian movement, to renew an ageing ecclesiastical tradition."[12]

David Edwards is looking to such men as Dr. Robinson, the Bishop of Woolwich, for this movement, which is, in his opinion, what some call "religionless Christianity". It is a new deal for the enlightened humanist. A re-moulding of traditional Christian theology to suit the new age.

This movement of the Holy Spirit, with which this book is concerned, follows a very different line—though equally dissatisfied with "religion" as such. It is the very antithesis to the *Honest to God* approach. It is a reassertion of the truth of the old theology and morality—but brought back to life again by the power of the Holy Spirit. It is an assertion that all the old Christian dogmas are true, but have become inert through unbelief and lack of experience by those that embrace them. As the *Living Church* article continued: "We know that we are members of a Church which desperately needs jarring, so that its thick crust of complacency may be shattered and that it may be freed to do the enormous tasks to which God has called it."[11]

D. L. Moody, the famous nineteenth century evangelist, as a young man had just given what he thought was a good talk. As he left the platform an old man stopped him. "Young man," he said, "when you speak again, honour the Holy Ghost." That stray remark lodged in the memory of the young man. Hurt at the time he afterwards was thankful for the reproof. Some years later he experienced the Baptism in the Spirit. The prime weakness of the Church today is its failure to "honour the Holy Ghost". How can we seek to know more of the truth and glory in our theology, when we do not honour the Spirit of truth—sent by the Son to lead us into all truth? As we face the facts of our need, how can we ignore a movement which speaks directly to them? We must look more closely at the two most distinctive doctrines and practices of it—the Baptism in the Holy Spirit and the gifts of the Spirit.

The Baptism in the Holy Spirit

At the present time the whole Church is reconsidering Christian initiation. The relationship of the Holy Spirit to this is obviously important. If the expression "Jesus is Lord" was an early Christian creed or affirmation of faith, then we can see the importance of the Holy Spirit, for according to Paul "no man can say Jesus is Lord *except by the Holy Spirit*" (1 Cor. 12.3).

In the Church of England there are two main views about confirmation and its relationship to water baptism. The first links the coming of the Holy Spirit more or less exclusively with water baptism, while the second links it more with confirmation. Other churches, which do not practise the rite of confirmation, have roughly the same difference of opinion. For instance, there is a growing practice in Baptist churches of laying hands on candidates immediately after they have been baptised.

In view of the neglect of the doctrine of the Holy Spirit since the days of the early Church, it is not really surprising that misunderstanding and divergent thought and practice have developed. But let us now go back to the original pattern of the New Testament and see if we can discover the answer.

From the Day of Pentecost onwards the presence of the Holy Spirit was a potent factor in the life of the Church. This cannot be overstressed. Men and women were being initiated in those days into a community of people who had a deep awareness and experience of God by the Holy Spirit. They would, therefore, have known at once if their own experience measured up to that of others. The milieu of most churches today is very different. Many Christians would have virtually to admit that they have "never even heard if there is a Holy Spirit". Others know something *about* the Holy Spirit, but have very little experience of His power and influence in their lives.

So on the Day of Pentecost itself the crowd knew exactly what Peter meant when he told them that they would receive the gift of the Holy Spirit. They had just seen for themselves the effect this had had on the gathered

Church, and in amazement had asked the question—"What meaneth this?" They had heard uneducated simpletons speaking fluently languages they had never learnt, but which they had been able to recognise. Some had thought they were drunk, but others were greatly struck by what they had heard and seen.

The receiving or Baptism of the Holy Spirit was thus part of normal Christian initiation right from the beginning. As we go into this subject more thoroughly, certain interesting facts emerge. The first is that nowhere is the coming of the Holy Spirit coincidental with water baptism. Even in the experience of Christ at the river Jordan, the descent of the Holy Spirit followed His baptism. This was the normal order of events in those early days, and the Church for many years attached a great deal of importance to the experience of Christ at His baptism in the river Jordan. At Pentecost, therefore, the crowd was told that if they were baptised they would receive the gift of the Holy Spirit.

Later, when Philip preached in Samaria, the Holy Spirit came to the converts some time after they had been baptised, for the apostles Peter and John had to come down from Jerusalem to pray with them and lay their hands on them.

In Paul's case we do not know whether he was baptised before or after he had received the Spirit. So also was the case of Cornelius and his friends at Caesarea, but in this instance the coming of the Holy Spirit alone convinced Peter and his friends that they should go ahead and baptise the first Gentiles.

When Paul spoke to the disciples in Ephesus—again we see the coming of the Holy Spirit *after* their baptism.

At first sight there does not seem to be a clear consistency in all these examples. But there is one way in which this apparent confusion may be resolved. It is when we see the main work of the Holy Spirit in the life of the individual as two actions and not one. There are many people who see His work as one single action called regeneration. In this action men and women are made the children of God or, in other words, are brought into membership of the Body of Christ. If this were so, then both the Samaritan and Ephesian believers in the examples given in the Acts of the Apostles were baptised as unbelievers—for they were only "regenerated" after they had been baptised. But this is foreign to the whole idea of baptism in the New Testament. No, there does seem to be this further action of the Holy Spirit, which is quite distinct from His act of regeneration, and which is bestowed upon believers. Again—in the New Testament this action is always described as coming "upon" rather than "in" the believer. In this action the Holy Spirit empowers those who are already members of the Body of Christ.

Thus we can summarise the New Testament position in this way. It was first expected that men and women should repent and believe on the Lord Jesus Christ. This itself was only possible through the agency of the Holy Spirit. Then the quiet work of regeneration would be effected by the Holy Spirit and the new convert would be baptised in water forthwith. They would also be taught to expect the Holy Spirit to come upon them as they were leaving the baptismal waters (as in the case of Christ) or after the application of hands by the elders of the church. In New Testament days, as we shall see later, this was normally accompanied by speaking in tongues, which was both the consequence of the Holy Spirit's descent, and also the sign of His power.

At all events—something definite was expected to happen, so that when Paul asked the question, "Did you receive the Holy Spirit when you believed?" he expected a definite answer—"Yes" or "No".

Bishop Cockin in his book on the Holy Spirit *God in Action* has written of this incident: "Why is that somewhat brusque question Paul's first remark to them? There can surely be only one answer. They didn't look as if they had. Something was missing that ought to have been there, something that men were beginning to look for as a distinctive mark of those who had had the characteristic vitalising experience of becoming Christians ... There is no mistaking the fact that something had happened. A spring, as it were, was released; there was an inner response to the

99

touch of a divine power. Does anything comparable happen to most of us at confirmation? And would it be a good thing if it did? It sets one thinking."[13]

It certainly does set one thinking. There is not time here to trace the vicissitudes through which Christian initiation has passed since those early days. But suffice it to say that at a very much later date the same pattern is still discerned.

For instance, Cyril of Jerusalem, writing in the fourth century, likened Christian initiation to the experience of Christ at Jordan—"as the Holy Spirit in substance lighted on Him, like resting upon like, so, after you had come up from the pool of the sacred waters, there was given to you an unction, the antitype of that wherewith He was anointed, and this is the Holy Spirit."

And Tertullian, one of the most brilliant Christian scholars of any age, writing at the end of the second century and beginning of the third, says: "Not that in the waters we receive the Holy Spirit, but cleansed in water, and under the angel, we are prepared for the Spirit."

Augustine of Hippo as late as the end of the fourth century expresses the same view in two of his sermons. In the first he says: "When you were exorcised you were, so to speak, ground. When you were baptised you were, so to speak, watered. When you received the fire of the Holy Spirit you were, so to speak, baked."

And in the other. "This distinction between the reception of baptism and the reception of the Holy Spirit shows us clearly enough that we should not think that those whom we do not deny to have received baptism forthwith have the Holy Spirit."

The full evidence of the Church Fathers is most confusing—revealing that there was no definite view during this period. But these three quotations will show that this interpretation given of the New Testament passages was held by some for a considerable time after the apostolic age. The Church would do well to recognise the debt it owes to Pentecostals, in spite of all their theological ignorance, for bringing light to bear on this subject. They saw the primitive usage as a pattern for all time—applied it to themselves, with the results we have seen. It is true that it is dangerous to accept a doctrine solely on the grounds of experience. But doctrine *without* experience is dangerous also. The Pentecostals have demonstrated to our churches that experience should normally follow the correct application of scriptural doctrine. This should lead us to a greater clarification of the theory and practice of Christian initiation.

Throughout the Middle Ages and the Reformation period there was little attention given to the subject of the Holy Spirit. The Puritans were less guilty of neglect—and perhaps the greatest book ever written on the subject of the Holy Spirit came from the pen of a Puritan—John Owen. But Owen and others tended to concentrate on the work of the Holy Spirit in regeneration. However, in the works of another Puritan, Thomas Goodwin, there is a most interesting discussion of the subject. It comes in his lengthy commentary on the Epistle to the Ephesians when he comes to expound the meaning of the text "after that ye believed ye were sealed with the Spirit of Promise". The writer regarded this "sealing of the Spirit" as a work of the Holy Spirit which normally follows regeneration and baptism and is to be distinguished from them. His teaching here is analogous to that of the Baptism in the Spirit; in fact in one place he calls it this: "The seal of the Spirit is called 'baptising with the Holy Ghost' because it is that which is the fruit of baptism." He quite clearly distinguishes this work of the Spirit from that of regeneration. "It is not to work regeneration, but supposeth it."

To Goodwin it was normally received in New Testament days, but had been lost sight of in his own. "Thus ordinary it was in the Primitive times—where the defect lies, God knows." But he goes on to urge Christians to seek it: "It might be more common if men would sue it out ... you that believe are to wait for this Promise ... Sue this Promise out, wait for it, rest not in believing only, rest not in assurance by graces only, there is a further assurance to be had—it was the last legacy Christ left upon earth ... sue out the will of Christ, sue out that last legacy of His. It was the fruit of His ascension—when He was ascended up and received this Promise, then He poured it out...."

One of the greatest Anglicans was Charles Simeon. For more than fifty years Vicar of Holy Trinity Church, Cambridge, in the eighteenth century, more than any other man he helped to shape Evangelical convictions. He was virtually the father of the Evangelical party in the Church of England. There is not a wealth of teaching about this aspect of the Holy Spirit in his writings, but he does follow Thomas Goodwin regarding the matter of the "sealing of the Spirit". He viewed it as something which comes after conversion and is only given to those who seek it. Such people he writes, "must first be 'in Christ' and then for Christ's sake this benefit should be vouchsafed to them." But he acknowledged that in his day there were many to whom this teaching was "mere foolishness." He rebukes them for speaking evil "of things that they understand not", and goes on to urge them to "seek to experience it, instead of censuring those who do".

D. L. Moody was a staunch expositor of what he unashamedly called "the Baptism in the Spirit". In a sermon he referred to the day of Pentecost in this way: "Now I believe the gift of the Holy Ghost that is spoken of there is a gift for certain but one that we have mislaid, overlooked and forgotten to seek for. If a man is only converted and we get him into the Church, we think the work is done—and we let him go right off to sleep—instead of urging him to seek the gift of the Holy Ghost that he may be anointed for the work ... The world would soon be converted if all such were baptised with the Holy Ghost."

But were the Pentecostals right in adding "tongues" to the doctrine of the Baptism in the Holy Spirit? It was especially this which caused them so much persecution, and which led to division and strife.

If we examine the New Testament evidence, there is a far stronger case for this than people at first sight imagine. In the Acts of the Apostles we can obviously only take as examples those cases where the receiving of the Baptism in the Spirit is actually described. We cannot deduce anything, for instance, from the 3,000 who were converted on

102

the day of Pentecost, as we are only told they were baptised in water. The Holy Spirit is not mentioned, although He was promised to them if they repented and were baptised. It is always dangerous to argue from silence, unless there is some indication from other evidence. We are not told either how Paul was filled with the Holy Spirit through the ministry of Ananias, although we do know from his own pen that he spoke in tongues. We are, therefore, left with only four occasions when the Baptism in the Spirit is described in the Acts (Acts 2:4, 8:17, 10:44, 19:6). In three of these it is clearly stated that they all spoke in tongues when the Spirit was given. In the fourth incident there is a clear inference that they did, although the fact is not actually stated. This is the case of Peter and John's visit to Samaria. When they laid their hands on the Samaritan Christians something very definite must have happened, because the magician Simon Magus, who was watching, *saw* it. What did he see? It must have been something very obvious for a man like him to offer money to have the power to reproduce it.

Morton Kelsey writes: "In view of the other passages from Acts the gift Simon wanted to be able to use was *unquestionably* glossolalia. It is an impressive experience to witness a spontaneous outpouring of tongues and it is certainly one that would interest Simon, a magician who was trading on the supernatural."[14]

It does look very much as if "speaking in tongues" normally accompanied this experience in the early Church. If someone says—"But what about other gifts of the Spirit?" the answer is—this is the only one ever mentioned (apart from prophecy which is linked with it in Acts 19:6). And it is clear that on these occasions *all* those who received the gift "spoke in tongues".

The rest of the teaching about glossolalia in the New Testament bears this out. The only reference in the Gospels tells us that this gift would "follow *them that believe*" (Mark 16:17). The other signs mentioned are also promised to the same category of people—healing, exorcism and immunity from poison, and may be experienced when necessary. Again, in 1 Corinthians 14, Paul suggests that "speaking in tongues" is for every believer. This inference can be drawn from the purpose for which the gift is bestowed—"speaking to God" and "edifying to oneself". It can also be seen in the desire of the apostle that they all should speak in tongues. If reference is made to 1 Corinthians 12: 30—where Paul asks the question, "Do all speak with tongues?" and expects the answer "No"—then we must examine the context of chapters 11–14 carefully. Paul is here describing the proper functioning of the local congregation. In this verse he is not thinking so much about the private devotional use of tongues, as the public use in the church for edification—with, of course, interpretation. In the *public* use of this gift it is clear that not all will speak in tongues. But *privately* all may, at least that is the wish of the apostle who counted it a personal blessing himself.

This argument may not satisfy some. But at least we should recognise that there is a case for this linking of the Baptism in the Spirit with speaking in tongues. It has been loyalty to this conviction which has in the main cost Pentecostals so much ridicule and condemnation. Now some theologians are coming to see that they have been right all along.

The Gifts of the Holy Spirit

Although Pentecostalism has been dubbed "the Tongues Movement", it has really stood for the importance of the other gifts quite as much as that of tongues. Here they are as Paul gives them to us (1. Cor. 12: 7-10):

The utterance of wisdom
The utterance of knowledge
Faith
Gifts of healing
Working of miracles
Prophecy
The ability to distinguish between spirits
Various kinds of tongues
The interpretation of tongues

104

At first sight a strange assortment indeed. It is important at the outset to realise that Paul is not talking about *natural* talents or faculties. Paul calls these—the "spirituals"—and so they are. They are given by the Holy Spirit irrespective of merit or human ability. They are not given for *permanent* exercise—but as and when necessary for the benefit of others. One of the best definitions of these gifts is given by the Puritan divine, John Owen, who distinguished carefully between what he calls "ordinary" and "extraordinary" gifts. The latter he describes as: "Such as absolutely exceed the whole power and faculties of our minds and souls. They did not consist in an abiding principle or faculty always resident in them that received them so that they could exercise them by virtue of any inherent power and ability. They were so granted unto some persons in the execution of their office as that so often as was needful they could produce their effects by virtue of an immediate extraordinary influence of Divine Power transiently affecting their minds."

There are surely many times when natural reasoning and intuition is not enough—when the finest education and training is insufficient; then the Holy Spirit will give, if we will only believe, the utterance of wisdom or knowledge—or the ability to distinguish spirits. This is analogous to the promise of Christ to His disciples that the Holy Spirit would do this for them in an emergency: "Settle it, therefore, in your minds not to meditate beforehand how to answer; for I will give you a mouth and wisdom which none of your adversaries will be able to withstand or contradict" (Luke 21: 14).

These gifts, as John Owen has said, are not permanent—like natural gifts—but transient—"a flash of inspiration" as we might call it. They are bestowed by the Holy Spirit on members of the Body of Christ when they are needed for the edification and welfare of others.

But now—are Pentecostals and others justified in saying that all these gifts are intended to be operative in the Church today? Or were all or some of them purposely withdrawn by the Holy Spirit after a certain time had elapsed? This is an important question to settle in our minds, otherwise our discussion of the subject will be purely academic.

Certainly on the face of it we must take seriously the claims of many balanced sensible Christians inside the denominations as well as in the Pentecostal churches to have known and experienced all these gifts in recent years. But we obviously cannot allow the matter to rest there. They all could have been deluded. Now, there have been many views expressed on this subject—but briefly they can be divided into three. The first view is that these gifts were intended for the early Church alone. Those who claim to exercise them today are, however sincere, self-deceived. The second is that, although not permanently withdrawn, they are manifested at the sole discretion of the Holy Spirit, who may decide to withdraw them for one age and restore them for another. The third view is that these gifts were intended ideally for the Church throughout its earthly pilgrimage, and will only be withdrawn at the return of Christ. Their absence in the Church for much of its history is explained by the lack of faith and knowledge of them.

Which view is right? The first view has in recent years lost much support. It is very largely based on the idea that the gifts of the Spirit were given as a kind of scaffolding before the erection of the building itself. When the Church became established the scaffolding of the gifts was removed. It is also linked with the idea that the gifts were temporary means of instruction before the New Testament had been written. And so when this work was completed there was no longer any need for them—especially perhaps the gift of prophecy.

If we look closely at these arguments we shall detect weaknesses in them. It is incorrect surely to think of the Church as a permanent structure—in its earthly aspect—around which scaffolding is erected. Every generation is a new Church of living souls—still needing all the protection, support and help that God can give. The Church has never been "established". It never will be in this sense until the Church militant here on earth is merged finally with the Church triumphant in heaven.

An American layman has put it like this: "It is presumed that what is meant is that in early days glossolalia was needed as a crutch to the Church, but now the Church is strong and no longer needs the crutch. Therefore, whether glossolalia is authentic or not is not at issue. The entire controversy boils down to the fact that some authorities feel the Church has so matured as to be able to discard such manifestations of the Holy Spirit ... Truly it is difficult to imagine anyone, be he theologian, priest, bishop, or a mere layman, who could possibly consider that in matters involving God and religion we, as mortals, are anything other than infants or cripples."

Concerning the second argument: although the New Testament was not completed it is true until towards the end of the first century, yet most of the teaching contained in it was being currently used in the churches throughout this period—even though some of it had not yet been committed finally to writing. Immediately after Pentecost we are told that they continued "stedfastly in the apostles' doctrine". What was this? Surely the teaching of Christ given to the apostles by the Holy Spirit—much of which was later to become the New Testament. If anything in this period they had *more* teaching than we have—for they were very much closer to the earthly life of Christ than we are, and would have had more of His teaching. Paul, for example, quotes in his charge to the elders of Ephesus the words of Jesus, "It is more blessed to give than receive" as if they knew them. These words of course do not come in the Gospels. So we see that if the gifts were necessary in those days, they are still needed today.

Moreover, there is no statement in the New Testament which would lead us to believe that Christ or the apostles regarded the gifts as temporary. Indeed the only passage which deals with this teaches the exact opposite. In 1 Corinthians 13 Paul contrasts some of the gifts with the graces—faith, hope and love. He teaches that while these graces are permanent, the gifts are temporary—they are going to pass away. But the question is—when? Paul fortunately tells us—"when the perfect comes". Most scholars are agreed that Paul is here referring to the return of Christ, when the gifts will be withdrawn *because they will no longer be necessary.* This indicates surely that the gifts were intended for the whole of church history until Christ returns. If the gifts are to be withdrawn before then—logically "knowledge" also will be, for Paul links this with gifts. No theologian would be happy about that supposition.

The second view is more commonly held. It does not assert that the gifts have been permanently withdrawn—but it blames their absence from the Church on the Holy Spirit, who has withdrawn them *pro tem*. Thus the gifts, which are sovereignly controlled by the Holy Spirit, are quite unpredictably given or withheld by Him. It is natural that those with a Calvinistic leaning tend to take this view. It seems to have been the opinion of John Owen, who did not think that his own day was intended to be favoured by the Holy Spirit with "extraordinary" gifts. But he does not say that a later generation might not be blessed with such gifts. For instance, after asserting that there was no certain time for the cessation of these gifts he adds: "It is not unlikely but that God might on some occasions for a longer season put forth His power in some miraculous operations, and so He may yet do and perhaps doth sometimes . . ."

This was also the view of Charles Simeon. In one of his famous sermon outlines he says: "I think then, we may say, that learning must supply the place of miracles, unless God should be pleased to restore to His Church those powers which for so many centuries have been withdrawn."

The weak point of this argument is seen when we look again at the New Testament. In the Mark 16 passage Christ told his disciples that some of these gifts would follow "them that believe". There is no suggestion here that the gifts would be limited to special seasons. In 1 Cor. 12: 31 Paul urges the Corinthians earnestly to desire the higher gifts. In 1 Cor. 14: 1 he goes further and tells them earnestly to desire the spiritual gifts—especially prophecy. Are we to understand from this that Christians are to have an *earnest* desire which can never be satisfied because the gifts have been withdrawn by the Holy Spirit? If so, then it runs contrary to the whole of God's dealings with His people—for He never commands us to do anything which He will not enable us to fulfil.

The only view which accords with both the New Testament and church history is that these gifts were intended for the Church until the return of Christ, and were only withdrawn because of the faithlessness and ignorance of the Church. This is the view which John Wesley held. Writing about the Montanists he said: "The grand reason why the miraculous gifts were so soon withdrawn was not only that faith and holiness were well-nigh lost; but that dry, formal, orthodox men began even then to ridicule whatever gifts they had not themselves; and to decry them all, as either madness or imposture."

But there is a further question which needs answering. Granted that they are for today—how important are they? Are they not being given exaggerated prominence? Are they really necessary? It is obvious that the Holy Spirit would not give Christians unnecessary gifts. They must be important for Him to bestow them on the Church. The early Church thought them to be important enough. For instance, Paul exhorted Timothy not to neglect "the gift which you have which was given you by prophetic utterance when the elders laid their hands upon you" (1 Tim. 4: 14). This implies that it was possible to neglect this gift, and also that it was important not to do so. Also writing to the Thessalonians Paul urges them not to "despise prophesying". Again the suggestion is made that it was possible to underestimate the importance of this gift.

But why are they important? First, clearly, for the building up of the Church. They enable us to strengthen each other in the Lord. There is plenty of scope for this in the average church today. An edified church is much more likely to be a growing one. The gifts of the Spirit do also have an evangelistic potential. We need to remember that it was the speaking in tongues which drew that large crowd on the Day of Pentecost and captured their imaginations. A little later another huge crowd gathered when a lame man was healed at the gate of the Temple. Throughout the Acts we see these gifts being used as "signs" to the unbelieving world that Jesus was alive and His power available. Many were converted as a result. We are faced with a very similar situation today. Have God or His methods changed?

In this century we have seen amazing developments in the field of psychology and psycho-analysis. At the same time there has been a serious deterioration in mental health in this country. There is not time within the scope of this book to go into this important subject in any detail, but the gifts of the Holy Spirit have been proved to be truly relevant to it. Morton Kelsey in his book goes into this at some length.[15] He is well able to do so as he has done graduate work in psychology and studied for a time at the C. G. Jung Institute in Switzerland. The experience of the Baptism in the Spirit and speaking in tongues is proving in some instances to have a therapeutic value in mental illness. Far from driving people to psychologists, as some have claimed it does, it is delivering people from need of their services. Many people experience release from tension and inhibitions which leads to a more integrated and balanced life. And which of the most normal of us have not *some* part of our personalities out of the true? There is much scope in this field. One might not be far wrong in saying that, whereas the Pentecostal Movement has helped to make physical healing part of the life of a normal church— the new movement in the churches is spearheading a recovery of the power to lead others into mental and emotional healing—which itself, of course, relates to physical health.

But why have these gifts been so neglected down the centuries? We have seen part of the answer already. Another big factor has been the tremendous emphasis in Western Christendom on the mind and human reason— leaving little or no room for more direct inspiration. If it is thought that the mind has a monopoly in the realm of edification, then there is obviously no room for the gift of tongues—in which the mind, according to Paul, is "unfruitful". Here we see again the cleavage which has existed for so long between the Eastern and Western Churches. The former has allowed much more scope for the Holy Spirit and His more direct ways of inspiration, whereas the latter has emphasised reason and logic.

Another factor contributing to their neglect has been the excesses which have so often accompanied them, and the inability or unwillingness of the Church to distinguish between the true and the false. Irenaeus, writing at the end of the second century describes those "who mock the gifts of the Spirit". He goes on, "It is with them as with others, in order to get rid of false brethren they deny the whole brotherhood." It is always a mistake to throw the baby out with the bathwater. Or again Jonathan Edwards writing in the eighteenth century tried to defend the revival which had taken place in New England from the attacks of its critics, who were displaying that human weakness of "either approving or condemning all in a lump". It is much easier to do this—but surely we are called to exercise sober judgement, and with God's help distinguish carefully between what is of man and what of God.

To a growing number of discerning spectators this movement of the Holy Spirit is basically sound and healthy. Let Jonathan Edwards have the final word. To him the revival in his day was a glorious work of God. His critics thought otherwise and suggested that it displayed symptoms of insanity in those involved. Edwards' rejoinder was terse and to the point: "Now if such things are enthusiasm and the fruits of a distempered brain, let my brain be evermore possessed of that happy distemper!"

CHAPTER TWELVE

SEEING THE DANGERS

ROBERT MURRAY M'CHEYNE drew up a fine Bible reading system. In the introduction to it he discusses some of the dangers of it.

"If there be so many dangers," he says, "why propose such a scheme at all? To this I answer—that the best things are accompanied with danger, as the fairest flowers are often gathered in the clefts of some dangerous precipice."

There are a number of dangers to this subject which need to be recognised and carefully guarded against. But such dangers need to be set against the constant danger which faces the Church of the weight of mediocrity.

Morton Kelsey's stock answer to the question, "Isn't it dangerous?" is, "Yes, but isn't a dead church more dangerous than a dangerous one?" He goes on to say: "Dealing with the living God is a dangerous adventure. Jesus and Paul believed that there was malignant spiritual reality as well as good, and that it was dangerous. Man needed strong medicine to deal with it. For Jesus the Cross was strong medicine. In apostolic times, as Acts tell us, Ananias and Sapphira found dealing with God a deadly dangerous business. Spiritual reality has to be dealt with or it will deal with us, and tongues is, in one way, a strong medicine."[16]

No soldier goes into battle expecting it to be like a Sunday school treat. It is dangerous. He might be killed, wounded or captured by the enemy. He must take the risk or stay at the home base. Why should any Christian think it is going to be any easier? We too have a relentless foe. He is strong and has an army of spiritual beings behind him. He has a huge propaganda department bent on distorting the truth and sowing lies. He is implacable and unmerciful. He will never surrender. The early Church recognised this. Paul called it warfare and a wrestling match—demanding full concentration and all the weapons that God could provide.

It is interesting that the New Testament tells us that in the last days, although God would pour out His Spirit, Satan would also do his best to match that power. The activity of Satan would be "with all power and with pretended signs and wonders and with all wicked deception for those who are to perish".

Although it is important that we see the dangers in this subject, it must fairly be stated that in many churches people have been so consistently warned about these dangers that they have been frightened off the whole subject. We must be balanced here. Even when the gifts of the Spirit were being abused in Corinth Paul does not hesitate to urge Christians to seek them. But having faced the facts, we must examine the dangers. As Jonathan Edwards has wisely written—"a work of God without stumbling blocks is never to be expected."

Division

One of the main criticisms is that this subject causes division. "It's divisive," people constantly say. This must be fairly faced. But first we need to recognise the fact that division may not in itself always be wrong. We are three times told about Christ, for instance, "There was a division because of Him." Was He guilty of divisiveness? No, the guilt lay on the other side. Christ also told His disciples "Do you think I have come to give peace on earth? No, I tell you, *but rather division*." It takes two, usually, to cause a division, and it is superficial to suggest that because something causes a division it must therefore be wrong. We need to look more closely before we can arrive at a fair conclusion.

But having said this, it must be admitted that there is a real danger of every movement in the Church leading to division. There is also the eternal problem of *corruptio optimi pessima*. Bishop Cockin has written: "The pages of history show that the desire for a severer standard of morality, the aspiration towards a higher level of holiness,

113

can be distorted in ways which lead to results almost exactly the opposite of those which were intended." [17]

The writings of John Wesley abound in allusions to this problem which he himself had to face many times. "Beware of schism," he writes, "that inward disunion the members ceasing to have a reciprocal love 'one for another' is the very root of all contention and every outward separation. Beware of everything tending thereto. Beware of a dividing spirit; shun whatever has the least aspect that way ... suffer not one thought of separating from your brethren whether their opinions agree with yours or not. Do not dream that any man sins in not believing you, in not taking your word; or that this or that opinion is essential to the work, and both must stand or fall together. Beware of impatience of contradiction. Do not condemn or think hardly of those who cannot see just as you see, or who judge it their duty to contradict you whether in a great thing or a small.... Oh beware of touchiness, of testiness, not bearing to be spoken to; starting at the least word; and flying from those who do not implicitly receive mine or another's sayings!"

What sound and sensible advice! We shall deal more fully with the safeguards in the next chapter—but in conclusion it must be recognised that no change is ever painless; but we should try to make the pain as slight as possible.

Fanaticism

Undoubtedly this subject encourages fanaticism and will attract cranks and charlatans like bees round a honey-pot. The Pentecostal Movement was nearly wrecked by foolish extremists, and only wise and restraining leadership saved it from perishing in a welter of emotionalism. There will always be sensuous people looking for cheap thrills and exciting experiences. There will always be those who specialise in the bizarre and unusual and who will be drawn to such a movement. Jesus Christ experienced the same Himself. We are told "a multitude followed Him, because they saw the signs which He did on those who were diseased". Later that same crowd tried impulsively to make Him King. No wonder we are told that Jesus withdrew from such human adulation.

But the temptation to fanaticism is always near to the spiritual person. It was after Jesus had experienced His anointing with the Spirit that He was tempted by the devil to throw Himself recklessly down from the temple and to make bread out of stones to satisfy his natural desires. There are some who have fallen into this trap skilfully set for them by Satan without knowing it; they become a stumbling-block to others too.

John Wesley suffered many heartaches because of the foolish antics of some of his followers—who separated from him after they had lapsed into fanaticism. He quaintly called it "London enthusiasm". Preaching in the North of England in June 1763 he found that the fanatics in London had already harmed the people he was visiting. "The wildness of our poor brethren in London has put it out of countenance above 200 miles off; so these strange advocates for perfection have given it a deeper wound than all its enemies together could do!"

It is quite easy to see how this subject lends itself to fanaticism. The fanatic does the most outrageous things— and then says, "God told me to do it". He oscillates from one "leading" to another. He claims the confirmation of dreams, voices, visions and prophecy for the most irrational behaviour. He becomes hurt and offended when anyone tries to correct him. So dissension enters the fellowship and one evil leads to another, and it is very difficult to deal with.

John Wesley aptly described fanaticism as "expecting the end without the means". He goes on to expand on this: "The expecting knowledge without searching the scriptures, and consulting the children of God; the expecting spiritual strength, without constant prayer and steady watchfulness; the expecting any blessing without hearing the Word of God at every opportunity." One might add to this list—the expecting signs and wonders without strict obedience to the will of God; expecting guidance without allowing time to wait upon God. The danger is obviously very applicable to those who believe in the operation of spiritual gifts, and the promise of power through the Holy Spirit.

Some texts have been used to attempt to justify fanaticism. One of the favourites is, "You do not need that any man should teach you." With the help of this text people will reject the advice of friends, and follow their own leading. But the basis of fanaticism is really pride. A really humble person may make many mistakes, but he will never become fanatical. John Wesley called fanaticism "the mother of pride".

The Pentecostal Movement has probably suffered as much as Wesley did from its unwise promoters. The shrewd advice of James in his Epistle is "the wrath of man worketh not the righteousness of God". We need also to take seriously the advice of Paul—"the Lord's servant must not be quarrelsome but kindly to everyone, an apt teacher, forbearing, correcting his opponents with gentleness". The Holy Spirit, as David du Plessis has put it, is not a "fighter". He does not browbeat or brainwash people into all truth. He leads them. He is not pictured as a lion "seeking whom he may devour"—but as a harmless dove. The moment we start forcing what really is our own will, the Holy Spirit has gone and we are on our own. The fanatic is not bothered about motives or methods. He gets on with it. He tends to be unscrupulous. Now all this is foreign to the Spirit of Christ, but alas, not to this subject.

It is possible for people to crave for emotional pleasure, which weakens rather than strengthens them, and leads to greater instability than ever. All this shows how potentially dangerous this subject is, and how neglect of the proper safeguards can cause harm both to individuals and the Church in general. But by and large the Church today is not in danger of a surfeit of emotion. "We have lots of room to move in," as Dennis Bennett has put it.

There is another danger in the development and practice of harmful techniques. This is especially true concerning praying with people for the Baptism in the Spirit, and the conduct of prayer meetings in which the gifts of the Spirit are manifested. Here some Pentecostals have erred in being over-zealous, and have offended people. It is as wrong to

116

use pressure techniques when praying with people for the receiving of the Holy Spirit as it is when urging them to accept Christ. A great deal of harm has been done by trying to work people up emotionally until their will-power is weakened and they give way—to what? It is really a form of brainwashing and an immoral technique in a Christian context. Praying with people is often a help, and the laying on of hands is scriptural—but the use of pressure is harmful and may even at times be dangerous.

Deception

The New Testament is full of warnings about the dangers of deception. When we move into the supernatural realm we are more liable to be deceived than before. Satan is very cunning, and can even disguise himself as an angel of light. There are evil spirits whose chief weapon is deception, and how gullible they often find Christians! God's people today have a reputation for credulity. They will swallow most things apparently without asking too many questions. Every confidence trickster knows that when he finds a Christian, he has found a sure victim. Just tell him a sentimental story and the Christian will believe him, and never question the honesty of the person. How much easier for demons trained in the school of the "father of lies"? If we realise that every one of the gifts of the Spirit can be counterfeited by Satan, we recognise the fact that there is a large area for deception. It is sad to see some church people dabbling unashamedly in spiritism—unaware of the serious danger they and others are in. Blithely, they answer, "As long as we are sincere, we are quite safe." What match are such people against lying spirits—and the principalities and powers behind them? They are guilty of flagrant irresponsibility.

But there are safeguards against deception in the supernatural realm. There is armour which can cover and protect us against the worst that the enemy can do. There are weapons God will give us to uncover the lies and deceptions of Satan. There are safeguards which we *must* apply in this matter if we are to survive.

CHAPTER THIRTEEN

APPLYING THE SAFEGUARDS

WE have seen some of the dangers to recognise. The uncharitableness which leads to division. The pride which leads to fanaticism. The gullibility which leads to deception. How can we be safe from these harmful agencies, and still enjoy the benefits which the Holy Spirit wants to bestow upon the Church? The Corinthian Epistles are a reminder of what happens when Christians cease to love one another and become proud and arrogant. But most of the other Epistles of the New Testament imply that these dangers were averted by the proper application of the remedies—so that the full blessing was experienced—that which "makes rich and adds no sorrow to it".

The Word of God

This is the main safeguard—for God in His wisdom has given to the Church not only the inner testimony of the Holy Spirit, but also the outward one of the Scriptures. And the two agree. When they don't agree, something is wrong. For the Holy Spirit who inspired men to write the Scriptures will never lead people to disobey them or act independently of them.

The great danger at all times is lack of balance, and the Christian needs continually, without getting into bondage to it, to see that his life and conduct is balanced and sober. There is a necessity to embrace and obey "the whole counsel of God". Just as some are tempted to take their theological scissors and excise the chapters on spiritual gifts in the New Testament, so others are tempted to major on these very chapters and so neglect the rest of the Bible —as if spiritual gifts are the only matters worth being concerned about. This is all the more dangerous when these chapters become the subject of much controversy. People are tempted to spend far too much time discussing them.

But let us now see where the balance is needed. First, naturally, in our teaching and experience of the Trinity. The Church has often suffered from an emphasis on one or other of the persons of the Trinity—so that people become either unitarian or binitarian in experience if not in actual belief. To say that the Holy Spirit has been neglected is not to say that His person and work should now be given disproportionate attention at the expense of the Father and the Son. For the Holy Spirit's work is to glorify and manifest the Son and lead us to a true filial and intimate relationship with our gracious Father, who gave Him for us. For instance it is the Spirit who enables us not only to say "Jesus is Lord" but also "Abba, Father". But balanced teaching and experience should enable us to understand and appreciate the full glory and majesty of the Trinity in a meaningful manner.

Another area in which there should be careful balance is in the relationship between the edification which comes through the Bible and that which comes through spiritual gifts. In the New Testament we see them existing happily side-by-side. The gifts are there—not to replace the Word of God—but to confirm its power and message. The gifts are always to be brought to the judgement of the Scriptures as to a superior authority (see 1 Cor. 14: 29). The need for balance here is vital. There is a temptation, in the excitement of hearing and seeing the more spectacular manifestations, to emphasise them to the detriment of the authority of the Word of God. This is to court disaster. The safeguard is seen in the undoubted emphasis in the New Testament on teaching rather than spiritual gifts for the edification of the Church.

Some are worried about what will happen to the sacraments of the Church. Again it must be stressed that the gifts of the Spirit are not modern replacements for sacraments. Those who have experienced the blessing of the Holy Spirit and the operation of the gifts on the whole have a much higher regard for the sacraments than they ever had before. For some the dryness and formality of much of the Church's ritual and sacraments is removed and the services come alive with new meaning and power. But there is a danger, which must be guarded against, to throw over these things in favour of the gifts.

Everything must be brought to the touchstone of the Scriptures, which must obviously be more thoroughly and carefully read than ever before. The balance of them must be maintained. Mature and wholesome Christian living is the result of a careful balance between extremes. Freedom, for example, can drift into either bondage or licence. There can be too much concentration on evangelism to the detriment of the fellowship of believers. But equally there is the danger of a Christian group becoming a "holy huddle" and neglecting those outside its ranks. There can be too much emphasis on the spontaneous and unusual elements in worship and service—at the expense of the regular and normal disciplines, without which the whole thing can degenerate into emotional bedlam, as happened in the church of Edward Irving in the last century. The safeguard is the regular disciplined reading and exposition of all the Scriptures—not our pet passages. We see this exemplified in the Corinthian Church, where Paul confessed that he had fed them "with milk, not solid food" because they were not ready for this kind of teaching—they were "still of the flesh". A concentration on spiritual gifts can retard rather than advance the spiritual growth of Christians unless it is balanced with solid instruction in the whole counsel of God.

"You are in danger of enthusiasm," wrote John Wesley, "if you depart ever so little from Scripture; yea, or from the plain, literal meaning of any text, taken in connection with the context."

The Mind of Man

Again it is a matter of balance. As we have seen, there has been a tendency to emphasise human reason, and so to leave little or no room for the sudden and miraculous inspiration which may come to the mind through the agency of the Holy Spirit. But there is an equal danger that those who concentrate on this "extraordinary" inspiration, as John Owen called it, neglect, to their loss, human reason and the natural ability to "think through" matters presented to the mind—with the help of God of course.

John Wesley put it this way: "You are in danger of enthusiasm every hour—if you despise or lightly esteem, reason, knowledge, or human learning; everyone of which is an excellent gift of God and may serve the noblest purposes. I advise you never to use the words wisdom, reason, or knowledge by way of reproach. On the contrary, pray that you yourself abound in them more and more. If you mean worldly wisdom, useless knowledge, false reasoning, say so; and throw away the chaff but not the wheat."

To the mind unenlightened by the Holy Spirit Christianity seems unreasonable. But to the person whose mind has been enlightened it does become reasonable. But the Christian is not then to jettison his mind and its faculties as if they are useless in the spiritual realm. To do so is extremely dangerous and may well open the door to many vain delusions, which have led numbers of God's people seriously astray. We may be led by the Spirit to do things which on their face value appear unreasonable. But to God, who knows the end from the beginning, there is a reason for such guidance which will eventually be revealed. For instance, when Philip the evangelist was taken away from a very successful mission in Samaria to the desert places, it must have seemed unreasonable to him. But he obeyed, and soon discovered that there was a very good reason for this guidance.

In other words, God will never compel us to do things which are unreasonable—and we should beware of falling unwittingly into this trap. We are not to live "as the Gentiles do in the futility of their minds", but to "be renewed in the spirit of our minds"—and to be "mature in our thinking".

The Discipline of the Church

The Baptism in the Holy Spirit is given to unite not divide us from other Christians. "For by one Spirit we were all baptised *into one body*, Jews or Greeks, slaves or free, and all were made to drink of one Spirit," writes Paul

121

(1 Cor. 12: 13). This power is given not only that we might be effective witnesses to the world but also efficient members of the Body of Christ, the Church. The person blessed is not intended to be an isolated "power-house" for free-lance Christian activity—but a properly integrated member of a team. This makes it very much harder—and can result in friction and misunderstanding. The temptation will be for such a person to separate from the rest of the Church and run his own.

This raises the whole matter of division—how it is caused and how it may be prevented. The reason for division is never easy to find. But very often it is caused by the enmity which eternally exists between the flesh, or "self", and the Spirit. "The desires of the flesh are against the Spirit and the desires of the Spirit are against the flesh; for these are opposed to each other" (Gal. 5: 17). We see this contrast many times in the Bible, and it is usually the one "born after the flesh" who persecutes the one "born after the Spirit". Let us examine one or two illustrations of this. First, there are the sons of Adam, Abel and Cain. Abel was a man "of the Spirit", and Cain "of the flesh". Abel pleased God, Cain didn't. What happened? Cain murdered his brother in anger and jealousy. There is a definition of a religious fanatic—"a person who loves Jesus Christ more than I do". And the "fanatic" is persecuted—because the flesh opposes the Spirit.

Another illustration is that of Joseph and his brothers. Joseph was obviously more spiritual than they. His brothers were selfish and jealous. They were overwhelmed with jealousy and sold him into slavery. There was the same conflict between David and Saul. You can trace this factor as a thread throughout the Bible right down to the supreme example—the hounding of Jesus Christ Himself to death by men "of the flesh" filled with envy—the ugliness of whose lives was made only too evident by the peerless character and life of Christ. The flesh cringes from such devastating revelation.

Now it is important for us to realise that it does not always follow that those who have been filled with the Holy Spirit speak in tongues, and know experimentally the gifts of the Spirit are always in the category of "men of the Spirit"—and those who are unsympathetic are "men of the flesh". It is not quite as simple as that, and we would be making a big mistake to think it. We have only to go to the Corinthian letter again for this to be made plain. Here we see the same conflict—but the man "after the Spirit" is Paul, being persecuted and maligned by the Corinthians who were "still of the flesh" according to Paul, and yet "not lacking in any spiritual gift" and all "baptised in the Spirit".

Nevertheless this fundamental conflict between the flesh or human element and the Spirit or divine is at the basis of much division in the Church. The only way to resolve the tension is for all to "walk in the Spirit" and then there will be no "gratifying of the desires of the flesh". Then there will be no "self-conceit, no provoking of one another, no envy of one another" (Gal. 5: 16, 26).

This tension arises in a variety of practical ways. Christians after this experience will want to spend longer in prayer which will be more fully impregnated with worship and praise. They will be more concerned about obedience and moral rectitude. They will want to talk about the Lord and what He is doing in their lives, and so will become disinterested in frivolous and trivial conversation. They will exude Christian joy and peace more obviously and witness more boldly and freely. They will seek out kindred souls, which might mean weakening former friendships. All this may cause resentment in others who do not share the same experience. There may be the impugning of one another's characters. Then in those who have been blessed spiritual pride may gain the ascendency, and an arrogance which makes the whole matter many times worse. They begin to stand up for their "rights". They may make issues out of doctrine—*especially regarding the gifts of the Spirit.*

The minister finds himself in a difficult situation—a kind of "umpire" in a spiritual conflict. He wisely refuses to take sides. He ends up under strong attack from both sides. The one accuses him of being "unspiritual" in not encouraging the operation of the gifts, and the others of being "too soft" in dealing with this divisive element. So the situation can go from bad to worse.

There is no easy solution to this perennial problem in the Church. The final answer lies in the degree to which the whole Church is acquainted with holiness and the life of self-denial. But the Church of God will never be completely free from this type of problem this side of heaven.

Two extremes should be avoided at all costs. The first is the forbidding of the exercise of spiritual gifts in the Church and of course the excommunicating of those who manifest them. This is a step which Paul never resorted to, even under the strong provocation of the scandalous behaviour of the Corinthians. He states categorically, "Do not forbid speaking in tongues"—and he means in church as well as in private. The second extreme is to major on spiritual gifts and to make an issue of them in the church. The subject needs delicate handling. It will be new to most Church members. It may offend their aesthetic sense—and jar on their traditional understanding of worship, prayer and fellowship. They should be gently introduced to the subject—and thoughtfully considered. The subject should be seen in its proper perspective—in relationship to the rest of the "counsel of God". A difficult enough situation can be aggravated by these two extremes. If people are forbidden to do what Scripture allows, they will be tempted to the other extreme of over-emphasising the gifts. On the other hand, if people over-emphasise the gifts of the Spirit, others will be tempted to forbid their exercise.

It is obviously important that the minister and lay officials of the Church should exercise discreet discipline in this matter in order to keep it under control. The scriptural principles should be enforced—"Let all things be done for edification" and "All things should be done decently and in order" (1 Cor. 14: 26, 40). Both these principles, however, should be seen in relationship to the further injunction, "Do not quench the Spirit" (1 Thess. 5: 19). There is no reason why a local church should not be absolutely united in this adventurous quest for and enjoyment of the power of the Holy Spirit. In the present situation, although there have been unfortunate incidents, a number of churches are finding that where there is wise and strong leadership the results are good and wholesome to say the least.

One last point. The early Church apparently found it necessary to have "letters of recommendation" (2 Cor. 3: 1) as they were called. These were for those who had an itinerant ministry. This was to guard the local churches from the unscrupulous activities of false apostles, prophets and teachers, who even in those early days were passing from church to church deceiving the brethren. Something like this is still advisable today. Those who invite "unknown" people to minister in their churches should check their credentials first—for there are still "many false prophets who have gone out into the world". The ability to perform "signs and wonders" is no criterion to follow. The false prophet in the book of the Revelation is able to do this. Let us be "as wise as serpents" as well as "harmless as doves".

The Holiness of the Believer

Dietrich Bonhoeffer has written: "When Christ calls a man—He bids him come and die." There is a danger that in concentrating on Pentecost and the blessing that flows from that event one forgets or neglects the Cross and all its benefits. For some the Cross is of such supreme importance that Pentecost might never have taken place. To such people the death of Christ is the answer to all our needs, so that they have unconsciously come to regard the coming of the Holy Spirit as more or less superfluous. Such a view does scant justice to the teaching of Christ Himself and the apostles, who obviously regarded Pentecost and the work of the Holy Spirit as of immense significance.

But there is an equal danger in thinking of Pentecost and the Baptism in the Holy Spirit as the answer to everything. The death of Christ is thus removed from its central position which it should hold in the thought and experience of the believer. Without a clear understanding of this the church which opens its doors to the Holy Spirit in this new way will be in for a hard time. There are few things which appeal more to the selfish element in the Christian than "power". This was the downfall of the Corinthian church.

We have seen already how the answer to the "flesh"—which is another word for "self"—is to "walk in the Spirit". Paul goes on to say, "Those who belong to Christ Jesus have crucified the flesh with its passions and desires." If we belong to Christ, then we have renounced all that is ours—our reputation, our will, our plans, our whims and fancies—everything. This is what it means to "deny ourselves"—to take up the Cross daily, and to follow Christ. There are Christians today who know very little of this kind of life. These are the ones who use the gifts of the Spirit as if they are toys and abuse the privileges and the responsibilities of power. The Holy Spirit desires that Christ should be seen and heard, but we are often like those Corinthian Christians—followers of men—boosters of personalities. To walk in the Spirit means to deny "self", and we cannot have it both ways. We died with Christ 2,000 years ago. And faith in this great truth is as vital for Christians as the complementary truth that Christ died for us is for unbelievers. A fellowship composed of people concerned solely with the glory of God and the good of their neighbours is the best soil for the sowing of the Holy Spirit's power and gifts. The other kind of soil leads to problems at once.

The greatest safeguard against improper use of power is—love. This is why Paul makes much of it in the letter to the Corinthians—devoting a whole chapter to it. It is important to notice that Paul is not presenting love as an alternative to spiritual gifts—but as its proper and essential motive. "Make love your aim," he writes, "*and* (not *or*) desire the spiritual gifts" (1 Cor. 14: 1). The point of the hymn of love in Chapter 13 is to show that there is a "more excellent way" of manifesting gifts than the one the Corinthians were following. Because of their self-interest they were blind to the needs of others. Their desire for gifts was in order to enhance their own reputations rather than care for the needs of others. This, Paul says, should be the supreme motive—the good of others. We should want the gifts in order to be better equipped to help others.

So love should never be a substitute for gifts—but its supreme motive. It should also be the greatest safeguard

126

against the abuses and dangers we have mentioned. It will not be a naive kind of love—but the variety spoken of by Paul which "abounds more and more *with knowledge and all discernment* so that you may approve what is excellent and may be pure and blameless for the day of Christ" (Phil. 1: 9–10). It will not be human love, but that which is the principal fruit of the Holy Spirit.

John Wesley saw how many mistakes were made because of the neglect of love: "Another ground of these, and a thousand mistakes, is, the not considering deeply that love is the highest gift of God—humble, gentle, patient love; that all visions, revelations, manifestations whatever, are little things compared to love; and that all the gifts above mentioned are either the same with or infinitely inferior to it.

"It were well you should be thoroughly sensible of this —the heaven of heavens is love. There is nothing higher in religion—there is, in effect, nothing else; if you look for anything but more love, you are looking wide of the mark, you are getting out of the royal way ... you can go no higher than this till you are carried into Abraham's bosom."

Perhaps it is true to say that love is one of the main marks of this movement—rather than "speaking in tongues" which captures most of the publicity. Christians are receiving a deeper love for God and His Son—a richer love for other Christians which is bringing together men and women of very different traditions—and a broader love for all men and desire for their good. If this is so, then it deserves both success and sympathetic interest.

REFERENCES

All biblical references are made in the text, and are taken from the American Revised Standard Version.

[1] p. 22: Mgr. Trouncer, *Miser of souls*, p. 201.
[2] p. 33: *The Pentecostal Movement* (Allen & Unwin, 1964), p. 181.
[3] p. 45: *Pentecostalism and Speaking with Tongues* (Highway Press, 1964), p. 9.
[4] p. 45: *The Pentecostal Movement* (Assemblies of God Publishing House), p. 89.
[5] p. 46: ibid., p. 89.
[6] p. 47: ibid., p. 58.
[7] pp. 78, 79: *Saturday Evening Post,* © 1964 by the Curtis Publishing Co. Used by permission.
[8] p. 79: *Speaking with Tongues* (Epworth Press, 1965), p. 120.
[9] p. 94: *Pentecostalism and Speaking with Tongues*, p. 7.
[10] p. 95: *Speaking with Tongues*, p. 95.
[11] pp. 95, 96: *Living Church*, July 17th, 1960. Used by permission.
[12] p. 96: *The Honest to God Debate* (S.C.M. Press, 1963), p. 15.
[13] p. 100: F. A. Cockin, *God in Action* (Penguin Books, 1961), p. 46.
[14] p. 103: *Speaking with Tongues*, p. 30.
[15] p. 110: ibid., chapter 7.
[16] p. 112: ibid., pp. 227-8.
[17] p. 114: *God in Action*, p. 108.

PSEU-DO CHRISTIANS by Dr. Ray Jarman A516/95¢
The dangers of liberal and occult
teaching in lives of Christians and non-Christians.
Dr. Jarman for 50 years was a leader in science of the mind
religions until a dramatic conversion at 70 years of age.

THIS EARTH'S END by Carmen Benson A513/95¢
The Bible contains prophecy telling how this earth
will end. This is a clearly written, easy to understand
explanation of dreams and visions in the New Testament.

JESUS AND ISRAEL by Carmen Benson A514/95¢
The Old Testament revealed through dreams and visions
the future happenings on the earth. An accurate account
of things to come.

WALK IN THE SPIRIT by Michael Harper L319/95¢
Renewal or Revolution — The Church must decide. Some have
discovered a new dimension in living through God's power.

GONE IS SHADOW'S CHILD by Jessie Foy L337/95¢
A moving story of a mother's faith in God for
her son and of a highly effective B10-chemical
treatment called megavitamin in schizophrenia.

SPIRITUAL WARFARE A505/95¢
A practical study on demon oppression and exorcism.
A positive method in freeing the oppressed.

GOD'S JUNKIE by Sonnie Arguinzoni
with Jouinn Ricketts A509/95¢
Introduction by David Wilkerson
A former junkie (his story is in Run Baby Run)
tells of the unique addict church — "Miracles do
happen" by Nicky Cruz.

HEAR MY CONFESSION by Fr. Joseph E. Orsini
L341/95¢ A Roman Catholic priest tells his
personal story of how he discovered the Catholic
Pentecostal experience.

THERE'S MORE L344/1.50

RUN BABY RUN by Nicky Cruz L-101/95¢
The true story of a gang leader turned crusader.

THE LONELY NOW by Nicky Cruz
with Jamie Buckingham A510/95¢
Nicky answers the questions youth ask.

THE CHALLENGING COUNTERFEIT
by Raphael Gasson L102/95¢
Hidden secrets of spiritualism disclosed by a former medium who tells how to know the real.

ANGELS OF LIGHT? by Dr. Hobart Freeman A506/95¢
Dr. Freeman reveals the source of power in the popular occult practices and the deliverance from them.

EMOTIONAL ILLS AND THE CHRISTIAN
by G.J. Guldseth, M.D. A507/95¢
A high percentage of illness is attributed to the psychosomatic. Dr. Guldseth discusses ways of healing through the Bible.

PRISON TO PRAISE
by Chaplain (LTC) M. Carothers A504/95¢
Revolutionary concepts in achieving remarkable answers to problems through praise.

THE SPIRIT BADE ME GO
by David du Plessis L-325/95¢
A charismatic journey of one man bringing him before thousands in a world-wide ecumenical mission for the Holy Spirit.

WISE UP! HOW? by Clinton White L-318/95¢
"I was an alcoholic fourteen years and addicted to drugs. I was set free. I call it a miracle."

- -